The Compl...
Festive V...
Recipes

Jean Conil

The Complete Book of Festive Vegetarian Recipes

Jean Conil

foulsham

LONDON • NEW YORK • TORONTO • SYDNEY

foulsham

Yeovil Road, Slough, Berkshire SL1 4JH

ISBN 0-572-01815-0

Phototypeset in Great Britain by Typesetting Solutions, Slough, Berks.
Printed in Great Britain by St Edmundsbury Press Ltd., Bury St Edmunds, Suffolk.

Contents

Introduction   7

Basic Vegetable Preparation
& Cooking   10

1 Celebration Soups   13

2 Vegetarian Sauces   25

3 Starters   39

4 Assorted Salads   57

5 Light Meals or Starters   75

6 Pasta and Rice Dishes   101

7 Egg Dishes   129

8 Pulses   149

9 Potato Dishes   169

10 Chinese Celebration Stir Fry
Dishes   185

11 Celebration Desserts
and Cakes   199

Index   249

Introduction

Taste for centuries has totally dominated our choice of food. It is only in recent years that the public has become aware of the need to consider the healthy aspects of our diets. All kinds of gastronomical tricks have been exalted, even up to the level of awarding medals for "best looking dish of the nouvelle cuisine class". However, the real revolution in our kitchens has been far more scientific and given more prominence than any other artistic considerations.

Eating good food together with others is however still a social event. In this book, Festive Vegetarian, the celebration of a birthday, or wedding or the enjoyment of a party is as important as preparing a meal for Christmas, New Year or Easter feasts.

It does not take much imagination for a cook to produce a palatable meal with the large resources of our international vegetable and orchard gardens. The supermarkets and Asiatic stores are well furnished with enormous varieties of pulses, sprouts for salads, exotic fruits and unusual vegetables. Aubergines and peppers are grown in England and successful attempts have also been made to grow soya beans.

Our natural and nutritious foods have for too long been debilitated and subjected to all sorts of synthetic colourings, stabilizers and emulsifiers, and now we are paying the price with the increase in allergies and other medical conditions. Interest in natural and untreated foods is growing with an increased protest against harmful additives and expensive food processing.

But while we do not proscribe entirely the use of convenience foods, we must consider more carefully

what is most useful in our everyday cooking. The stock cube has its benefits in saving the time of lengthy stock-making, as do the vegetable yeast extracts needed to complement the B group vitamin. One can use white flour as well as wholewheat flour without detriment to our health. The daily fibre intake needs of most people can be met by eating one apple a day and consuming unpeeled tomatoes, cucumbers, aubergines, peppers and other fruits like plums, peaches, cherries, apricots and pears, to name but a few. The daily need for vitamin C is well satisfied in the drinking of 300ml/½ pint/1¼ cups of freshly pressed citrus fruits. Vitamin C is lost in cooking, so eating raw fruits and crudities makes sense.

In the vegetarian world, salads lead the field in popularity especially when complemented with protein foods such as cheeses, eggs, pulses and cereals. Many books could be produced on the range of recipes available, exploring the entire repertoire. In our modest way we show you the main menu items which you could have every day without becoming aware of a monotonous repetition. From starters to desserts, the choice of a good meal is yours, coupled with enjoyment and contentment in being a true vegetarian.

Jean Conil

Basic Vegetable Preparation And Cooking

* All green vegetables should be washed in plenty of water to draw out any insects, then well drained in a colander.

* All salad leaves should be washed similarly, but after draining they should be patted dry on a clean tea towel.

* All root vegetables should be washed before and after peeling.

* New potatoes should start in boiling salted water, old potatoes in cold water. The size determines the length of time for boiling.

* Sliced and diced potatoes can be boiled in 5 minutes.

* Large baked potatoes will take 1 hour wrapped in foil. It is best to groove a line around the potato before baking, so that when it is cooked it will cut easily into halves.

* Aubergines (Eggplants) can be fried in the skin for better flavour. First sprinkle the cut aubergines with salt for 10 minutes to draw the bitter juices or soak them in cold water with a little vinegar.

* Spinach tastes best when stir fried in butter for 4 minutes. Or blanched for 2 minutes, drained, well pressed to eliminate surplus moisture, then reheated in butter.

* Green vegetables, peas, beans should be blanched for 4 minutes. Refresh in icy water to retain their green colour.

* The modern method of quick stir frying helps vegetables retain maximum flavour.
* Potatoes roasted in butter have a better colour and flavour than those baked in oil or dripping.
* All dried vegetables are better soaked in distilled water than hard water which lengthens the cooking time.
* The shape, size and cut of vegetables will determine their appearance and cooking procedure.

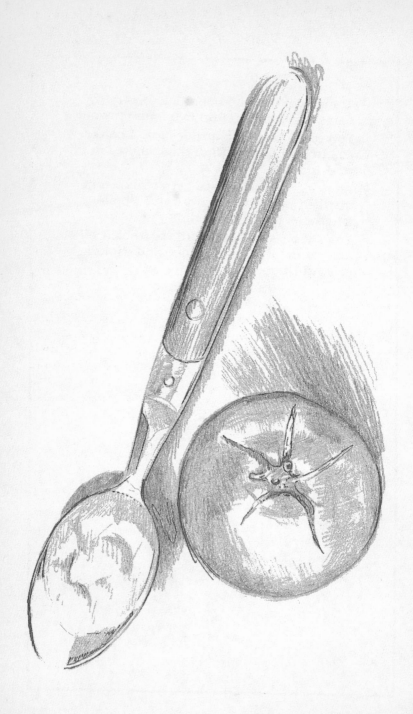

— CHAPTER ONE —

Celebration Soups

* * * * * * * * * * * * * * * * * *

In our Western world we celebrate with cold drinks but rarely with soups, yet sharing a bowl of hot steaming soup on a cold winter evening has been a tradition in many countries for a very long time. The country peasants of central France lace their soups with wine, the Scandinavian fishermen with aquavit and the Germans with beer. In the Pacific Islands, fermented coconut drinks are served in their shells as a symbolic cold soup. In modern French and British cuisine we still flavour our rich broths with Madeira wine. In this section I have made up a few soups using fruits and alcohol suitable for summer or winter festivities.

Avocado and Tomato Soup

Serves 4
Preparation 8 minutes
No cooking

	Metric	Imperial	American
Avocado, ripe	1	1	1
Medium tomatoes, skinned, seeded and chopped	2	2	2
Honey	1 tbsp	1 tbsp	1 tbsp
Juice of orange	1	1	1
Juice of lemon	1	1	1
Water or dry white wine	300 ml	½ pint	1¼ cups

1 Peel the avocado and scoop out the pulp. Place in the blender with tomato pulp, honey, orange, lemon juice and water or wine. Blend the mixture to a purée.

2 Serve chilled.

This popular cold soup gains from being left to mature in the refrigerator for two days. During the summer a larger quantity can be made as it will keep well for up to a week.

Lemon and Egg Soup

Serves 4
Preparation time 8 minutes
Cooking time 15 minutes

	Metric	Imperial	American
Olive oil	2 tbsp	2 tbsp	2 tbsp
Small onion, chopped	1	1	1
Carrot, chopped	1	1	1
Celery stalk, chopped	1	1	1
Water	600 ml	1 pint	2½ cups
Vegetable stock cube	1	1	1
Juice and grated rind of lemons	2	2	2
Egg yolks	3	3	3
Cornflour (cornstarch) blended with 45 ml/3 tbsp water	1 tbsp	1 tbsp	1 tbsp
Salt, pepper and sugar			
Lemon grass or coriander, chopped	1 tbsp	1 tbsp	1 tbsp

1 Heat the oil in a saucepan and stir fry the vegetables without browning for 3 minutes. Add the water and stock cube and boil for 8 minutes. Strain or liquidize. Reheat the soup to boiling point.

2 In a bowl combine the lemon juice, grated rind, egg yolks and blended cornflour. Pour approximately one cup of the hot soup into this mixture, stirring gradually, then add the blended lemon mixture to the remaining soup. Bring to the boil and simmer for 4 minutes. Season to taste and sprinkle with lemon grass or coriander. Serve with pitta bread.

15

Mexican Gazpacho with Chilli

Serves 4
Preparation time 10 minutes
No cooking

	Metric	Imperial	American
Red pepper, seeded and chopped	1	1	1
Tomatoes, skinned, seeded and chopped	2	2	2
Cucumber, sliced but not peeled	½	½	½
Clove of garlic	1	1	1
Small red onion, chopped	1	1	1
Green chilli, seeded and chopped	1	1	1
Slices of stale bread	4	4	4
Water	300 ml	½ pint	1¼ cups
Wine vinegar	3 tbsp	3 tbsp	3 tbsp
Olive oil	2 tbsp	2 tbsp	2 tbsp
Sugar	1 tsp	1 tsp	1 tsp
Salt	2 tsp	2 tsp	2 tsp
Fried croûtons to garnish			

1 Place all the ingredients in a 2 litre/3½ pint/4½ pint earthenware container with a lid.

2 Leave to marinate for two days in the refrigerator, during this time the mixture will ferment slightly and mature. The soup can be kept in the fridge for one week. Blend to a purée and chill. Serve cold with a garnish of fried croûtons.

Apple and Beetroot Wine Soup

Serves 6
Preparation 10 minutes
Cooking time 15 minutes

	Metric	Imperial	American
Walnut or sunflower oil	3 tbsp	3 tbsp	3 tbsp
Small onion, chopped	1	1	1
Small carrot, chopped	1	1	1
Small beetroots (beets), peeled and chopped	2	2	2
Fennel stalk, chopped	1	1	1
Water	600 ml	1 pint	2½ cups
Vegetable stock cubes	2	2	2
Garnish			
Beetroots (beets) boiled in the skin	2	2	2
Apples, cored, peeled and cut in strips	2	2	2
Red wine	150 ml	¼ pint	⅔ cup
Salt and black pepper			
Sugar (optional)	1 tsp	1 tsp	1 tsp

1 Heat the oil in a saucepan and stir fry the vegetables until lightly browned. Pour in the water and add the stock cubes. Boil for 8 minutes.

2 Peel the cooked beetroots, slice and cut into matchsticks. Marinate the beetroot and apples in the wine for 8 minutes.

3 When the soup is ready, add the beetroot and wine mixture to the hot soup. Simmer for 4 minutes. Season to taste, adding a little sugar if liked. Serve with hard-boiled eggs, cut into wedges, and brown bread.

Raisin Soup with Yoghurts

Serves 4
Preparation time 6 minutes
No cooking

	Metric	Imperial	American
Seedless grapes	100 g	4 oz	1 cup
Seedless dry raisins	50 g	2 oz	⅓ cup
Water	300 ml	½ pint	1¼ cups
Dry white wine	150 ml	¼ pint	⅔ cup
Small carton of plain yoghurt	1	1	1
Sugar	1 tsp	1 tsp	1 tsp
Ground cinnamon	¼ tsp	¼ tsp	¼ tsp

1 Combine all the ingredients in a blender and liquidize to a soft pourable purée. Serve chilled with cream crackers.

Garlic Soup of Provence

Serves 4
Preparation 8 minutes
Cooking time 12 minutes

This soup has wonderful therapeutic properties against flu.

	Metric	Imperial	American
Olive oil	3 tbsp	3 tbsp	3 tbsp
Cloves of garlic, peeled	12	12	12
Potatoes, peeled and diced	225 g	8 oz	2 cups
Water	600 ml	1 pint	2½ cups
Thickening			
Egg yolks	2	2	2
Cornflour (cornstarch)	1 tbsp	1 tbsp	1 tbsp
Milk	150 ml	¼ pint	⅔ cup
Salt and pepper			
Coriander leaves			

1 Heat the olive oil in a saucepan and stir fry the garlic without browning for 30 seconds. Add the potatoes and water. Boil for 8 minutes until the potatoes are tender. Pass through a sieve or blender. Reheat the purée.

2 In a bowl combine the egg yolks and cornflour blended with the cold milk. Pour in a cup of the warm soup and stir well. Add this mixture to the remaining soup. Simmer for 4 minutes, stirring continually. Season to taste. Sprinkle with coriander leaves and serve with sippets of bread.

Beer Soup With Sweet Onion

Serves 4
Preparation 8 minutes
Cooking time 10 minutes

	Metric	Imperial	American
Walnut oil	3 tbsp	3 tbsp	3 tbsp
Large red onion, chopped	1	1	1
Flat brown beer	300 ml	½ pint	1¼ cups
Water	300 ml	½ pint	1¼ cups
Sugar	1 tsp	1 tsp	1 tsp
Salt and black pepper			
Pinch of grated nutmeg			
Sippets of brown bread	50 g	2 oz	½ cup
Cheddar cheese, grated	3 tbsp	3 tbsp	3 tbsp

1 Heat the oil in a soup pan and gently fry the onion until golden. Add the beer and water, then boil for 10 minutes. Season to taste, adding sugar and nutmeg as well.

2 Place in four bowls and top with bread sippets and grated cheese. Brown under the grill (broiler) until cheese has melted.

Note: Sippets are slices of French bread baked in the oven. Croutons are small cubes of bread which are fried.

Peanut and Pumpkin Soup

Serves 4
Preparation 8 minutes
Cooking time 12 minutes

This soup can be garnished with boiled rice added at the last minute — 15 ml/1 tbsp per person.

	Metric	Imperial	American
Peanut oil	3 tbsp	3 tbsp	3 tbsp
Medium onion, chopped	1	1	1
Carrot, diced	1	1	1
Small green chilli, seeded and chopped	1	1	1
Celery stalk, diced	1	1	1
Pumpkin, cut into cubes	225 g	8 oz	1½ cups
Toasted peanuts	100 g	4 oz	¾ cup
Water	600 ml	1 pint	2½ cups
Tomato purée	1 tbsp	1 tbsp	1 tbsp
Vegetable stock cube	1	1	1
Dry Madeira wine	150 ml	¼ pint	⅔ cup
Salt, black pepper and grated nutmeg			

1 Heat the oil in a saucepan and stir fry all the vegetables, including the peanuts, for 4 minutes. Add the water, tomato purée and stock cube. Boil for 8 minutes.

2 Strain or liquidize in a blender. Add the Madeira wine. Reheat. Season to taste.

— CHAPTER TWO —

Vegetarian Sauces

* * * * * * * * * * * * * * *

There is one essential rule for cooks involved in the preparation of vegetarian meals, which is never use any fish, fowl or flesh of animals, this also applies to not using chicken or meat extracts. Vegetarian sauces are divided into four distinct groups:

* Made with dairy products — milk, cheese, eggs.
* Made with fruits — tomato, peppers, plums etc.
* Made with vegetables or herbs — mushrooms, beans, onions etc.
* Made with any kind of nuts — coconut, peanuts, almonds etc.

The texture of the sauce can be altered either by using the pulp of the main constituent as a purée (good for fibre) or by including starch-flour, cornflour, potato starch or other roots or cereals. The amount of starch needed is never more than 4 per cent of the liquid used, ie for 600 ml/1 pint/2½ cups milk, 24 g/scant 1 oz of starch would be enough. If a purée is used then the amount of starch can be reduced by half.

The seasoning is also very important, as a rule the salt content should not exceed 1 per cent or, for example, for 600 ml/1 pint/2½ cups of liquid, 1 level teaspoon at the most, and pepper should be a pinch per 600 ml/1 pint/2½ cups. Fresh chilli peppers can be used instead of peppercorns, 2 slices per 600 ml/1 pint/ 2½ cups using some of the seeds for strength. Red chillies are stronger.

Fresh spices should be used and ground when required. Good quality ground spices can be used but their flavour will be less fragrant. Of course many seeds are also used to great advantage, such as caraway, cumin, celery, anis seeds.

Dairy White Sauce

Serves 8
Preparation 5 minutes
Cooking time 8 minutes

	Metric	Imperial	American
Butter	25 g	1 oz	2 tbsp
Plain flour	25 g	1 oz	¼ cup
Milk	600 ml	1 pint	2½ cups
Small onion, sliced (optional)	1	1	1
Salt, white pepper and grated nutmeg			

1 Melt the butter in a saucepan and add the flour. Cook for 30 seconds without browning, stirring. Cool.

2 Boil the milk with the onion if using. Gradually add the milk to the roux, stirring to avoid lumps. Simmer the sauce for 3 minutes with the onion. Strain, then season to taste.

Variations (per 600 ml/1 pint/2½ cups):

Mixed herb: Add 2 tbsp chopped fresh parsley and basil.

Mushroom: Add 100 g/4 oz/1 cup white mushrooms, sliced and reheated in the sauce.

Onion: Add 1 chopped onion, boiled separately, to the white sauce. Strain, sieve or leave in the sauce.

Cheese: Add 50 g/2 oz/½ cup of any kind of hard cheese.

Egg: Add 2 egg yolks mixed with 100 ml/4 floz/½ cup single (light) cream. Stir into the cold white sauce. Reheat gently until hot, stirring.

Nutty White Sauce

Serves 8
Preparation 5 minutes
Cooking time 15 minutes

	Metric	Imperial	American
Almonds, chopped	100 g	4 oz	1 cup
Water	600 ml	1 pint	2½ cups
Sugar	½ tsp	½ tsp	½ tsp
Salt			
Cornflour (cornstarch) blended with 4 tbsp cold water	2 tsp	2 tsp	2 tsp
Grated nutmeg or ground ginger			

1 To make nut milk, place the almonds in water, sugar and salt in a pan. Simmer for 10 minutes. Liquidize and strain through a muslin cloth.

2 To thicken it, reboil. Stir the blended cornflour into the boiling almond milk. Simmer the sauce for 3 minutes. Check seasoning, adding grated nutmeg or ground ginger.

Variations: (per 600 ml/1 pint/2½ cups)

White mushroom: Add 100 g/4 oz/1 cup white mushrooms to boiling sauce. Simmer for 5 minutes. (The mushrooms can be sliced or chopped.)

Coconut: Add 100 g/4 oz/1⅓ cups desiccated (shredded) coconut.

Nutty Brown Sauce

Serves 8
Preparation 8 minutes
Cooking time 24 minutes

	Metric	Imperial	American
Oil	4 tbsp	4 tbsp	4 tbsp
Medium onion, chopped	1	1	1
Medium carrot, chopped	1	1	1
Toasted peanuts	100 g	4 oz	⅔ cup
Tomato purée	2 tsp	2 tsp	2 tsp
Clove of garlic, chopped	1	1	1
Water	600 ml	1 pint	2½ cups
Yeast extract (Marmite)	1 tsp	1 tsp	1 tsp
Small sprig of thyme	1	1	1
Cornflour (cornstarch) blended with 45 ml/3 tbsp water	1 tsp	1 tsp	1 tsp
Salt and pepper			

1 Heat the oil in a saucepan and stir fry the onion, carrot and nuts for 4 minutes. Add the tomato purée and garlic and cook for 1 minute more.

2 Stir in the water, yeast extract and thyme. Bring to the boil and simmer for 15 minutes. Strain or liquidize.

3 Reheat in a clean saucepan. Add the blended cornflour and boil for 4 minutes to thicken. Season to taste.

Variations:

Mushroom: Heat 4 chopped field mushrooms in the boiling sauce for 2 minutes, or add sliced mushrooms.

Olive: Add 75 g/3 oz stoned (pitted) olives.

Madeira: Add 100 ml/4 floz/½ cup medium Madeira wine to the boiling sauce.

Plum Sauce

Serves 8
Preparation 10 minutes
Cooking time 5 minutes

	Metric	Imperial	American
Juicy Victoria plums, stoned (pitted)	100 g	4 oz	4 oz
Honey	1 tbsp	1 tbsp	1 tbsp
Basic brown sauce	500 ml	18 floz	2¼ cups
Mixed spices	1 tsp	1 tsp	1 tsp
Chilli, chopped	1	1	1

1 Boil the plums and honey for about 5 minutes. Liquidize to a purée.

2 Blend this purée into the brown sauce. Flavour with mixed spices and chopped chilli.

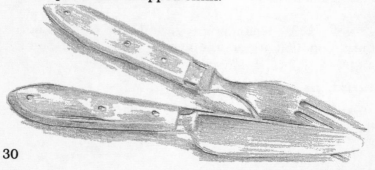

Red Bean Sauce

Serves 8
Preparation 8 minutes
Cooking time 13 minutes

	Metric	Imperial	American
Oil	2 tbsp	2 tbsp	2 tbsp
Cooked red kidney beans	150 g	5 oz	¾ cup
Clove of garlic, chopped	1	1	1
Yeast extract	1 tsp	1 tsp	1 tsp
Vinegar	1 tbsp	1 tbsp	1 tbsp
Chinese spice powder	½ tsp	½ tsp	½ tsp
Basic brown sauce	600 ml	1 pint	2½ cups

1 Heat the oil in a pan and stir fry the beans and garlic for 3 minutes. Add the yeast extract, vinegar, spices and brown sauce. Boil for 10 minutes.

2 Pass through a sieve and if too thick add either water or Madeira wine. Season.

Note: Both Plum sauce and Red bean sauce can be used with tofu dishes or any stir fried mushroom dishes.

Tomato Sauce

Serves 8
Preparation 5 minutes
Cooking time 18 minutes

Use for pasta and rice dishes.

	Metric	Imperial	American
Oil	4 tbsp	4 tbsp	4 tbsp
Medium onion, chopped	1	1	1
Clove of garlic, chopped	1	1	1
Medium tomatoes, coarsely chopped	4	4	4
Slice of red chilli	1	1	1
Water	600 ml	1 pint	2½ cup
Salt	1 tsp	1 tsp	1 tsp
Sugar			
Vegetable stock cube	1	1	1
Cornflour (cornstarch) blended with 3 tbsp water	1 tsp	1 tsp	1 tsp

1 Heat the oil in a saucepan and stir fry the vegetables for 4 minutes. Add the water and stock cube and boil for 10 minutes.

2 Season. Strain through a sieve or liquidize to a thin purée. Reheat to boiling point. Stir the cornflour and add to the hot mixture. Boil for 4 minutes to thicken and clear the starch.

Lemon Sauce

Use for mushrooms, tofu dishes, potato dishes and pasta.

Serves 8
Preparation 5 minutes
Cooking time 15 minutes

	Metric	Imperial	American
Water	600 ml	1 pint	2½ cup
Sugar	1 tbsp	1 tbsp	1 tbsp
Honey	1 tbsp	1 tbsp	1 tbsp
Lemon grass	1 tbsp	1 tbsp	1 tbsp
Vegetable stock cube	1	1	1
Turmeric	½ tsp	½ tsp	½ tsp
Ground ginger	½ tsp	½ tsp	½ tsp
Grated rind and juice of lemon	1	1	1
Thickening			
Vegetable margarine	25 g	1 oz	2 tbsp
Flour	15 g	½ oz	2 tbsp
Egg yolks	2	2	2

1 Boil the water with the sugar, honey, lemon grass and vegetable stock cube for 5 minutes. Add turmeric, ground ginger and grated lemon rind. Boil for another 3 minutes. Strain.

2 Melt the margarine in a saucepan and add the flour. Cook for 1 minute, stirring, without browning. Cool this paste and dissolve it in the hot sauce to thicken. Boil for 3 minutes and strain.

3 In a small bowl, mix the egg yolks with a cupful of the sauce. Add it to the remaining sauce. Bring to the boil and boil for 3 minutes. Lastly add the lemon juice. If added earlier the sauce would thin down. Season to taste.

Mayonnaise

Serves 8
Preparation 10 minutes
No cooking

	Metric	Imperial	American
Egg yolks	2	2	2
Salt	½ tsp	½ tsp	½ tsp
Pinch of white pepper			
Sweet made mustard	1 tsp	1 tsp	1 tsp
Lukewarm sunflower or peanut oil (arachide)	300 ml	½ pint	1¼ cups
Hot vinegar	1 tsp	1 tsp	1 tsp
Juice of lemon	½	½	½

1 Place the egg yolks in a bowl with the salt, pepper and mustard. Gradually, and in a small thread, pour in the warm oil, whisking in one direction only. As the sauce thickens, increase the flow of the oil until all is used.

2 Warm the vinegar and add it with the lemon juice.

Variations: (per 600 ml/1 pint/2½ cups of mayonnaise).

Pink dressing: Add 1 tbsp tomato ketchup and 1 tbsp Worcestershire sauce.

Tartare: Add 1 tsp chopped shallots, 1 tsp chopped capers, 1 tsp mixed fresh herbs and 1 small cocktail gherkin, chopped.

Mint: Add 1 tsp made mint sauce or 1 tbsp chopped fresh mint.

For salad dressings

Plain Salad Cream: Blend 300 ml/½ pint/1¼ cups cold white sauce, either Dairy or Nut, into 300 ml/½ pint/ 1¼ cups mayonnaise. Boil 1 tbsp vinegar with 1 tbsp sugar and add to the sauce. Adjust seasoning according to taste.

Yoghurt Dressing: Add 100 ml/4 floz/½ cup yoghurt to 300 ml/½ pint/1¼ cups mayonnaise. Sweeten the mixture with 1 tbsp sugar.

Creamier Dressing: Add 100 ml/4 floz/½ cup sour or double (heavy) cream to 600 ml/1 pint/2½ cups mayonnaise. Adjust seasoning with lemon juice.

Swedish Sauce: Add 100 ml/4 floz/½ cup apple purée to 600 ml/1 pint/2½ cups mayonnaise and 1 tbsp sugar.

Drinks On The House

There are no moral issues involved in not drinking alcoholic beverages with vegetarian meals. Festive gourmets will have a perfectly legitimate right to enjoy themselves during celebratory events.

Those who are more purists in their attitudes towards eating the vegetarian way may not wish to drink alcohol and would probably be happier drinking pure spring water and pure fruit juices. So in all the dishes listed in this book, vegetarians should please themselves.

However for those who may be interested in appreciating the wide choice of wines, ciders and beers from the entire world markets and will follow an old chef's guidance, here are a few suggestions.

* Cider and white wines go best with pasta and rice dishes.
* Beer and red wines with pulse dishes.
* As a rule you do not drink wine with salad containing vinegar.
* Red wine goes well with strong blue and fermented cheese.
* Vintage wines with semi-fermented cheese and the best Cheddars.
* Sherry and dry Madeira with light starters and cocktail snacks.
* Sweet wines and Champagne with desserts.

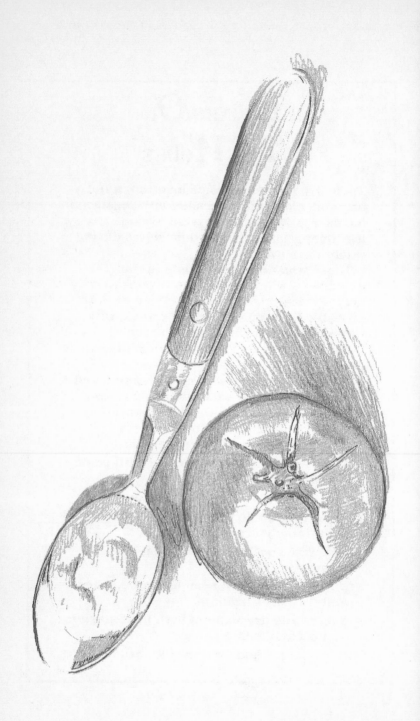

— CHAPTER THREE —

Starters

* * * * * * * * * * * * * * * * * * *

Light mousses or cooked purées form the basis of many of the starter dishes which are described in the following chapter. The mousse or purée can be flavoured with various seeds, spices or cream cheese.

A simple, but delicious paté can be made by sauteing a vegetable, for example aubergine or mushrooms, and adding eggs or cheese.

Stir-fried vegetables can be served hot or cold and make a tasty starter when served with a French dressing.

Aubergine Caviar

Serves 4
Preparation 10 minutes
Cooking time 5 minutes

	Metric	Imperial	American
Aubergine (eggplant)	1	1	1
Salt and black pepper			
Flour	2 tbsp	2 tbsp	2 tbsp
Sunflower oil	3 tbsp	3 tbsp	3 tbsp
Clove of garlic, chopped	1	1	1
Cream cheese	75 g	3 oz	6 tbsp

1 Cut the aubergine into slices, without peeling. Sprinkle with salt and leave for 30 minutes to allow the removal of the bitter juices. Wash, drain and pat dry. Sprinkle with flour and shake off surplus.

2 Heat the oil in a shallow pan and fry the aubergine slices for 5 minutes. Drain. Liquidize the aubergine to a purée with the garlic and what remains of the oil.

3 In a bowl, blend the aubergine purée with the cream cheese. Season to taste. Serve in individual ramekin dishes with toast.

Hummus –
Chickpea Caviar

Serves 4
Preparation 8 minutes
Cooking time 10 minutes

This is a rich protein vegetable pâté. Dry chickpeas (garbanzo beans) must be soaked in water overnight, then boiled for 1½ hours. Therefore it is often more practical to use canned chickpeas. In spite of the name, chickpeas are not a member of the pea family, known also by their Spanish name of garbanzos – they are a grain of the cicer aretinum family group.

	Metric	Imperial	American
Walnut oil	3 tbsp	3 tbsp	3 tbsp
Small onion, chopped	1	1	1
Water	100 ml	4 floz	½ cup
Fresh cooked or canned chickpeas (garbanzos beans)	225 g	8 oz	1⅓ cups
Yoghurt	75 ml	3 floz	6 tbsp
Salt and black pepper			
Tahini paste	2 tbsp	2 tbsp	2 tbsp

1 Heat the oil in a pan and stir fry the onion until golden. Add the cooked chickpeas and water. Boil for 5 minutes. Pass the mixture through a seive.

2 Blend the yoghurt into the purée and season to taste. Add the tahini paste. Serve with cheese crackers or vegetable crudities.

41

Hot Cheese and Potato Pâté With Herbs

Serves 4
Preparation 10 minutes
Cooking time 6 minutes

	Metric	Imperial	American
Potatoes, peeled and thinly sliced	225 g	2 tbsp	2 tbsp
Butter or olive oil	2 tbsp	2 tbsp	2 tbsp
Fromage frais	150 g	5 oz	½ cup
Salt and black pepper			
Chopped fresh herbs, such as parsley, chives, basil, thyme	4 tbsp	4 tbsp	4 tbsp
Juice of lemon	½	½	½

1 Boil potatoes for 6 minutes, drain and mash to a purée.

2 Combine with the remaining ingredients. Season to taste. Serve hot with cream crackers.

Carrot And Yoghurt Pâté Dip

Serves 4
Preparation 8 minutes
Cooking time 9 minutes

This honey flavoured carrot dip is one of the tastiest mixtures one can ever produce for celebration parties. Liked by all, old and young.

	Metric	Imperial	American
Walnut or sunflower oil	2 tbsp	2 tbsp	2 tbsp
Small onion, sliced	1	1	1
Young carrots, peeled and sliced	225 g	8 oz	8 oz
Honey	2 tbsp	2 tbsp	2 tbsp
Juice of lemon	1	1	1
Carton yoghurt	1	1	1
Salt and pepper			
Chinese or Cos lettuce leaves	4	4	4
Toasted almonds	2 tbsp	2 tbsp	2 tbsp
Orange, divided in segments	1	1	1

1 Heat the oil in a shallow pan or wok and stir fry the onion and carrots for 4 minutes. Add a cupful of water and the honey. Boil for 5 minutes until the carrots are soft.

2 Drain and mash the mixture coarsely. Blend in the yoghurt. Season to taste, add the lemon juice and rind. Serve on Cos or Chinese leaves. Sprinkle over toasted almonds and garnish with orange segments at the last moment.

Haricot Vert Medley

Serves 4
Preparation 10 minutes
Cooking time 10 minutes

One of the most popular combinations of flageolet and green beans has been served for centuries, both as an hors d'oeuvre or accompaniment. Served on its own, with an egg dressing, it is as nourishing as it is tasty to eat. Flageolets are available both dry and canned.

	Metric	Imperial	American
French beans, very thin, trimmed	225 g	8 oz	8 oz
Green flageolet beans	150 g	5 oz	5 oz
Spring onions (scallions), chopped	4	4	4
Egg dressing			
Hard-boiled eggs	2	2	2
Walnut oil	3 tbsp	3 tbsp	3 tbsp
Lemon juice	1 tbsp	1 tbsp	1 tbsp
Made mustard	½ tsp	½ tsp	½ tsp
Salt and black pepper			

1 Boil the French beans in salted water for 7 minutes. Drain and refresh in iced water for 5 minutes. Drain and pat dry.

2 If you use dry flageolets, soak them overnight and boil for 1½ hours in distilled water, as hard water takes longer. Otherwise use the canned variety and simmer for 10 minutes. Drain. Combine the two beans in a bowl.

3 For the egg dressing, separate the yolks from the whites of the eggs. Pass the yolks through a sieve and mix with oil and lemon juice. Add the mustard. Season to taste.

4 Toss the beans in this dressing. Sprinkle the chopped egg white on top of the salad with the chopped spring onions.

African Peanut Queen Dip

Serves 4
Preparation 5 minutes
Cooking time 3 minutes

The peanut is not really a nut but a vegetable plant producing a pod like peas and beans. The protein content is as rich as any animal source of protein. The fact that it has a fat content of 30 per cent has made it a good source of oil known as arachide oil. The so-called peanut butter is made by grinding the toasted peanuts to a cream to which two per cent salt is added. This dip has been spiced up and flavoured with coconut cream and honey.

	Metric	Imperial	American
Peanuts	225 g	8 oz	1½ cups
Honey	3 tbsp	3 tbsp	3 tbsp
Coconut cream (canned)	150 g	5 0z	½ cup
Salt to taste			
Pinch of chilli pepper			

1 Place the shelled peanuts on a tray and toast for 3 minutes. Grind them with a rolling pin, or a mortar or liquidize, with ½ cupful of hot water. Add the honey, coconut cream and seasoning and blend to a purée.

2 Serve with wedges of apple, pear, banana, peach or pineapple chunks. Ideal for childrens parties.

Pine and Basil Pistou Provencal Dip

Serves 4
Preparation 5 minutes
No cooking

This meridional paste has been used for soups, sauces and spaghetti for many years, less frequently it is served as a pâté spread on French bread. The French, who like outdoor parties laced with wine, have a taste for it. The pine nuts, known as Pinone nuts or Pignolia, are the seeds of the Stone pine. They are sold in Italy as desserts, but in the South of France many cooks use them with basil to flavour their fish soups. As a party dip the Pine pistou takes some beating.

	Metric	Imperial	American
Pine nuts	225 g	8 oz	2 cups
Basil leaves	6	6	6
Cloves of garlic	2	2	2
Walnut or olive oil	4 tbsp	4 tbsp	4 tbsp
White breadcrumbs	50 g	2 oz	1 cup
Fromage frais	50 g	2 oz	¼ cup
Boiling water (optional)	2 tbsp	2 tbsp	2 tbsp

1 In a mortar, pound all the ingredients to a fine paste. Add 2 tbsp boiling water for a smoother mixture.

2 Serve on toasted French bread.

Pepperoni Medley

Serves 4
Preparation 8 minutes
Cooking time 5 minutes

Mild peppers come in different colours, green, yellow and red. The red variety has most flavour. In this presentation hors d'oeuvre, the peppers taste better when lightly grilled and peeled.

	Metric	Imperial	American
Medium peppers of different colours	3	3	3
Oil, for frying			
Potato, peeled, sliced and cut in thin strips	1	1	1
Red onion, cut in strips	1	1	1
Fennel stalks, cut in thin strips	2	2	2
Dressing			
Olive oil	3 tbsp	3 tbsp	3 tbsp
Wine vinegar	1 tbsp	1 tbsp	1 tbsp
Clove of garlic	1	1	1
Salt and black pepper			

1 Cut the peppers in half and discard the seeds. Grill (broil) the peppers, exposing the shiny side. When it begins to blister, remove and peel the skin. Cut the peeled peppers in thin strips 4 mm/⅙ inch thick.

2 Fry the potato strips in oil for 1-3 minutes, without browning. Drain well. In a bowl, combine all the potato, onion and fennel strips with the peppers.

3 Mix the dressing ingredients with seasoning. Toss into the strips. Serve with hard boiled eggs, cut into wedges and lettuce leaves.

Cream Cheese and Leek Dip

Serves 4
Preparation 5 minutes
Cooking time 10 minutes

Leeks are considered by many gourmets to be the best vegetable after asparagus. The fact that they are cheap makes them the better choice as a flavouring in soups, etc.

	Metric	Imperial	American
Leeks, use white part only, sliced, about 225 g/8 oz	3	3	3
Butter	2 tbsp	2 tbsp	2 tbsp
Flour	2 tbsp	2 tbsp	2 tbsp
Milk	150 ml	¼ pint	⅔ cup
Fromage frais	100 g	4 oz	½ cup
Salt and black pepper			

1 Wash the sliced white part of the leeks in plenty of water. Drain and pat dry in a cloth.

2 Heat the butter in a saucepan and stir fry the leeks without browning. Sprinkle over the flour to absorb the butter and stir the cold milk into this mixture. Bring to the boil and simmer for 5 minutes.

3 Cool, then blend in the fromage frais and season to taste. Serve cold on toast or with crackers.

Asparagus Mousse with Toasted Almonds

Serves 4
Preparation 10 minutes
Cooking time 6 minutes

	Metric	Imperial	American
Asparagus, thin type	225 g	8 oz	8 oz
Spring onions (scallions), trimmed and sliced	3	3	3
Water	150 ml	¼ pt	⅔ cup
Powdered gelatine	2 tsp	2 tsp	2 tsp
Whipping cream	150 ml	¼ pt	⅔ cup
Salt, white pepper			
Celery salt			
Grated nutmeg			
Flaked almonds, toasted	75 g	3 oz	¾ cup

1 Scrape the asparagus lightly and cut into small pieces.

2 Boil the asparagus and spring onions in the water for 6 minutes.

3 Dissolve the gelatine in the hot liquid. Liquidize the mixture to a purée or pass it through a sieve with the liquid.

4 Cool. When completely cold, fold in the whipped cream and season with salt, pepper and nutmeg. Divide the mixture into individual moulds. Chill to set the mixture.

5 Turn out the mousses onto plates and sprinkle with flaked toasted almonds just before serving. Serve with crackers or toast.

Petits Oignons à la Grecque

Serves 4
Preparation 5 minutes
Cooking time 6 minutes

These delicious onions, pickled in sweet white wine, are a great favourite for cheese parties. One can never make enough of this party pickle.

	Metric	Imperial	American
Small onions, weighing 25 g/1 oz each	450 g	1 lb	1 lb
Sunflower oil	4 tbsp	4 tbsp	4 tbsp
Honey	3 tbsp	3 tbsp	3 tbsp
Wine vinegar	4 tbsp	4 tbsp	4 tbsp
Sweet white wine	300 ml	½ pt	1¼ cups
Tomato purée	1 tbsp	1 tbsp	1 tbsp
Stick of celery, thinly sliced	1	1	1
Stalk of fennel, thinly sliced	1	1	1
Salt and pepper			

1 Peel the onions. Heat oil in a saucepan and stir fry the onions until lightly coloured. Add the honey and caramelize a little for 30 seconds, then pour in the vinegar, wine and tomato purée.

2 Add the celery and fennel and boil for 6 minutes. Season and cool in its own liquor. Serve cold with the liquid. Use to accompany assorted hard cheeses – Cheddar, Emmenthal, Port Salut, etc.

Green Olive Pâté

Serves 4
Preparation 10 minutes
No cooking

Lovers of olives will like this type of vegetarian French pâté, also known as Oliviera. It is served at barbecue parties with salads and local cheeses.

	Metric	Imperial	American
Large green olives, stoned (pitted)	150 g	5 oz	1 cup
Green chilli, seeded and chopped	1	1	1
Spring onions (scallions), chopped	2	2	2
Pickled gherkins (dill pickles), chopped	2	2	2
Pickled capers, chopped	1 tbsp	1 tbsp	1 tbsp
Chopped fresh parsley or coriander leaves	2 tbsp	2 tbsp	2 tbsp
Cloves of garlic, chopped	2	2	2
Olive oil	2 tbsp	2 tbsp	2 tbsp
Fromage frais	100 g	4 oz	½ cup

1 Pound all the ingredients in a mortar to a paste. Alternatively, mince them or liquidize using 45 ml/3 tbsp boiling water.

2 Serve on toasted French bread, on Cos lettuce or with celery stalks.

Pawpaw Pecan Cocktail

Serves 4
Preparation 10 minutes
No cooking

Pawpaw is an oblong fruit rather like a large avocado but it has an orangey colour. It tastes like a cantaloup melon and is often served like a fruit with mango as its partner. These fruits are available in most supermarkets as most tropical countries are growing them for export. It contains an enzyme which helps in the digestion of protein foods. For this reason, it is ideal to serve with rich protein foods like nuts, pulses and cheese.

	Metric	Imperial	American
Pawpaws, ripe	2	2	2
Filling			
Fresh sweet grapefruit	1	1	1
Juice of lemon	1	1	1
Kirsch, Gin or Cointreau	2 tbsp	2 tbsp	2 tbsp
Cos or Chinese lettuce leaves	4	4	4
Chopped pecan nuts	4 tbsp	4 tbsp	4 tbsp
Fresh mint leaves			
Garnish			
Cocktail cherries	4	4	4

1 Peel and cut the pawpaws into slices, removing and discarding the black seeds.

2 Cut the grapefruit into segments. In a bowl, combine the pawpaw with the grapefruit segments. Sprinkle over the lemon juice and liquour of your choice.

3 Serve on lettuce leaves and sprinkle over the pecan nuts. Garnish with mint leaves and cocktail cherries.

Mushroom and Pepper Moulds

Serves 8
Preparation 12-15 minutes
Cooking time 20 minutes

	Metric	Imperial	American
Milk	600 ml	1 pt	2½ cups
Butter	50 g	2 oz	¼ cup
Flour	25 g	1 oz	¼ cup
Powdered gelatine	25 g	1 oz	1 oz
Salt and white pepper			
Eggs, beaten	4	4	4
Garnish			
Red pepper, seeded and diced	100 g	4 oz	1 cup
Green peas	100 g	4 oz	¾ cup
Butter	50 g	2 oz	¼ cup
Onion, chopped	50 g	2 oz	½ cup
White mushrooms, sliced	225 g	8 oz	2 cups

1 To prepare a chaudfroid sauce like a Béchamel, first heat the milk. In a pan, melt the butter, add the flour and cook for 1 minute, stirring. Stir in the milk gradually to avoid lumps. Dissolve the gelatine in the hot sauce. Season to taste. Remove from heat and cool. When cold, blend in the beaten eggs.

2 Blanch the red pepper and peas for 3 minutes, then drain.

3 Heat the butter in a pan and stir fry the onion and mushrooms for 2 minutes. Then add the blanched peas and peppers and gradually blend in the sauce away from the heat.

4 Fill individual pyrex 150 ml/¼ pint/⅔ cup well buttered moulds and bake in the oven at 180°C/350°F/gas mark 4 for 20 minutes until set like a custard. Serve hot or cold.

— CHAPTER FOUR —

Assorted Salads

* * * * * * * * * * * * * * * * * * * *

By definition a composite salad should always consist of a main protein ingredient if served as a main course. The fact that salads are always flavoured with a dressing acidulated with vinegar, wine or lemon juice in which cheese, nuts and eggs can be blended, makes them by nature rich in protein. In addition, most salad eaters like to have a garnish of eggs or cheese or vegetable of the pulses family – peas, beans, soya, lentils – or any kind of nuts. So a salad therefore can be both nourishing and tasty.

Tomato and Cucumber in Brandy Dressing

Serves 4
Preparation 8 minutes
No cooking

Steak Tomatoes weighing 100 g/4 oz are recommended
for this special recipe.

	Metric	Imperial	American
Large tomatoes, 100 g/4 oz each	2	2	2
Cucumber	1	1	1
Dressing			
Blue cheese, mashed	25 g	1 oz	¼ cup
Walnut or olive oil	3 tbsp	3 tbsp	3 tbsp
Juice of lemon	1	1	1
Brandy	3 tbsp	3 tbsp	3 tbsp
Salt and black pepper			
Sugar	1 tsp	1 tsp	1 tsp
Garnish			
Chicory (endive) leaves	8	8	8
Walnut halves	8	8	8

1 Slice the tomatoes. Slice the cucumber slantwise.
Arrange alternately in rows on two large plates. Place the
chicory leaves in the centre.

2 Liquidize the dressing ingredients in a bowl until smooth and creamy. Drizzle the dressing over the salad. Garnish with walnuts.

Courgette Pasta Salad in Basil Sauce

Serves 4
Preparation 8 minutes
Cooking time 14 minutes

This Italian style salad is made with pasta combined with lightly sauteed courgettes with shredded fennel. All the ingredients must be cut in small strips, the length of the short macaroni.

	Metric	Imperial	American
Short cut macaroni	150 g	5 oz	1¼ cups
Fennel, cut in small, thin strips	1	1	1
Courgettes (zucchini), sliced slantwise	2	2	2
Basil leaves, chopped	6	6	6
Cloves of garlic, chopped	2	2	2
Olive oil	3 tbsp	3 tbsp	3 tbsp
Juice of lemon	1	1	1
Salt and black pepper			
Single (light) cream	75 ml	3 fl oz	6 tbsp

1 Boil the macaroni separately for 10 minutes. Drain.

2 Heat the oil in a wok and stir fry the macaroni and fennel for 1 minute. Add the courgettes, basil leaves, garlic and seasoning. Toss for 1 minute. Stir in the cream and reheat for 30 seconds.

3 On four plates arrange assorted salad leaves. Serve piping hot on the salad leaves. Squeeze lemon juice over at the last moment.

Avocado and Rice Bean Salad

Serves 4
Preparation 8 minutes
Cooking time 20 minutes,
plus cooking beans.

Avocado by itself can be bland, but as a garnish it is a good salad ingredient. The acidity of a ripe mango helps to give more taste, but you can use mango chutney. Rice and black eye beans provide the main substance.

	Metric	Imperial	American
Black eye beans, soaked overnight	100 g	4 oz	⅔ cup
Long grain rice	100 g	4 oz	½ cup
Water	600 ml	1 pt	2½ cups
Salt and pepper			
Sauce			
Sunflower oil	3 tbsp	3 tbsp	3 tbsp
Medium onion, chopped	1	1	1
Curry powder	½ tbsp	½ tbsp	½ tbsp
Tomato purée	1 tbsp	1 tbsp	1 tbsp

	Metric	Imperial	American
Garnish			
Avocados, ripe, stoned and sliced	2	2	2
Mango chutney	2 tbsp	2 tbsp	2 tbsp
Tomatoes, skinned, seeded and chopped	4	4	4

1 Boil the black eye beans for 1½ hours. Refresh.

2 Boil the rice for 20 minutes, refresh in the cold water and drain.

3 Combine the cooked rice and beans. Season to taste.

4 Prepare a curry sauce. Heat the oil and stir fry the onion until soft, but not coloured. Add the curry powder and tomato purée and a cupful of water. Boil for 8 minutes, then strain or liquidize.

5 On four plates, arrange a mound of rice mixture. Pour curry sauce around. Garnish the top of the rice mixture with slices of avocado. In the centre place a spoonful of mango chutney. Serve the salad with a side plate of chopped tomato pulp.

Peacock Feather Fan of Carrots and Cucumber

Serves 4
Preparation 10 minutes
Cooking time 20 minutes

The main ingredient of this spectacular salad presentation is green lentils in grapefruit juice dressing. The garnish is provided by carrots and cucumber arranged to imitate the feathers of a peacock, with the help of a few hard-boiled eggs.

	Metric	Imperial	American
Green lentils	150 g	5 oz	⅔ cup
Dressing			
Olive oil	3 tbsp	3 tbsp	3 tbsp
Grapefruit juice	3 tbsp	3 tbsp	3 tbsp
Spring onions (scallions) or shallots, chopped	2	2	2
Honey	1 tsp	1 tsp	1 tsp
Salt and black pepper			
Garnish			
Large carrots	2	2	2
Cucumber	½	½	½
Hard-boiled eggs	4	4	4
Snipped chives			

1 Boil the green lentils for 20 minutes. Drain and cool.

2 In a cup, mix the salad dressing. Toss the lentils in the dressing while still hot.

3 Thinly slice the carrots slantwise 4 cm/1½ inches long. Scald in boiling water for 1 minute only.

4 Slice the cucumber slantwise the same size. Shell the eggs and cut into thin slices using an egg slicer.

5 On four plates arrange a row of carrot, cucumber and eggs to imitate the peacock feathers. In the centre spoon the lentils and sprinkle chives all over.

New Potato Salad

Serves 4
Preparation 10 minutes
Cooking time 20 minutes

	Metric	Imperial	American
New potatoes	450 g	1 lb	1 lb
Garnish			
Watercress leaves	150 g	5 oz	5 oz
Spring onions (scallions), chopped	4	4	4
Dressing			
Egg yolks	2	2	2
Salt and freshly milled black pepper			
Made Dijon mustard	½ tsp	½ tsp	½ tsp
Oil	3 tbsp	3 tbsp	3 tbsp
Sour cream	3 tbsp	3 tbsp	3 tbsp
Juice of lemon	1	1	1
Mixed salad leaves to serve			

1 Boil the new potatoes for 20 minutes. Peel while still hot. Cut in slices and place in a large bowl.

2 Wash, drain and pat dry the watercress leaves and add to the potatoes with the onions.

3 In a bowl, place the egg yolks with salt, pepper and made mustard. Whisk while adding the oil in a small thread until the mixture thickens. Then blend in the cream and lemon juice.

4 While still warm, toss the salad gently in this dressing. Divide between four plates adorned with mixed salad leaves.

Coleslaw with Pineapple and Cashew Nuts

Serves 6
Preparation 12 minutes
No cooking

In Britain, coleslaw consists too often of plain Savoy cabbage and carrots with a salad cream dressing. People forget that the Germans invented this salad, which is served every day summer and winter in all central European countries. The use of pineapple in my recipe has been a welcomed flavouring ingredient which brings its precious enzyme helping to digest protein.

	Metric	Imperial	American
White cabbage	450 g	1 lb	1 lb
Green apples	2	2	2
Red apples	2	2	2
Slices of fresh pineapple	4	4	4
Cashew nuts, chopped	4 tbsp	4 tbsp	4 tbsp
Dressing			
Sunflower oil	4 tbsp	4 tbsp	4 tbsp
Cider vinegar	2 tbsp	2 tbsp	2 tbsp
Roquefort cheese, mashed with a little cream	2 tbsp	2 tbsp	2 tbsp
Salt	1 tsp	1 tsp	1 tsp
Black pepper	¼ tsp	¼ tsp	¼ tsp
Caraway seeds	1 tsp	1 tsp	1 tsp
Sugar	1 tsp	1 tsp	1 tsp
Single or sour cream	1 tbsp	1 tbsp	1 tbsp

1 Separate the cabbage leaves, wash and pat dry. Cut in thin shreds or grate half the cabbage. If it is compact, use a grater.

2 Core, but do not peel the apples. Divide in four wedges and slice the wedges to produce triangular pieces.

3 Cut the fresh pineapple slices into thin julienne strips.

4 Combine the ingredients in a large mixing bowl.

5 In a smaller bowl, place the oil, vinegar, Roquefort cheese, salt and pepper, caraway seeds and sugar. Add cream and whisk the mixture well. Toss the coleslaw into this mixture. Serve on four plates. Lastly sprinkle over the chopped cashew nuts.

Chicory with Potato Salad

Serves 4
Preparation 8 minutes
Cooking time 20 minutes

The white chicory leaf, which the Belgians called witloof and the French endive, can be used in numerous ways. The leaves have a slightly bitter taste which can be modified by using lemon juice. The flavour is even more agreeable when chicory is boiled and refried in butter.

	Metric	Imperial	American
Chicory chicons	4	4	4
Juice of lemon	1	1	1
Butter and oil mixed	6 tbsp	6 tbsp	6 tbsp
Salt and black pepper			
New boiled potatoes, cut in thin slices	450 g	1 lb	1 lb
Grated Emmenthal cheese	2 tbsp	2 tbsp	2 tbsp

Garnish
Curly lettuce, oak leaves, plain green lettuce leaves and mustard and cress.

1 Clean and trim the outer root bases of the chicory but do not separate the leaves. Scoop out the bitter core. Boil for 12 minutes in salted water, to which half of the lemon juice has been added. Drain and press out the moisture.

2 Heat half of the butter and oil in a pan and shallow fry the chicons for 3 minutes on each side over a low heat to obtain a light brown colour. Season with salt and pepper.

3 In the same pan, toss the potatoes with more butter and oil until golden. Season to taste.

4 Place the chicons on a tray and sprinkle over the grated cheese. Brown under the grill (broiler) for 1 minute. Arrange the assorted salad leaves around the edge of four plates. Drizzle lemon juice over the leaves. Add the chicory and sautéed potatoes. Sprinkle with chopped parsley. Extra lemon dressing can be used if needed.

Citrus Fruits on Spinach and Bean Sprouts

Serves 4
Preparation 10 minutes
No cooking

Packed with vitamin C and iron, what more can you wish for a better diet? This nutritious salad can also be served with hard-boiled eggs.

	Metric	Imperial	American
Lime	1	1	1
Lemon	1	1	1
Tangerine	1	1	1
Oranges	2	2	2
Grapefruits	2	2	2
Red morello cherries, stoned (pitted)	150 g	5 oz	½ cup

Salad
Green lettuce, spinach leaves
  and handful of bean
  sprouts.

Dressing
Salt and pepper

Salted peanuts, coarsely chopped	3 tbsp	3 tbsp	3 tbsp
Walnut or peanut oil	3 tbsp	3 tbsp	3 tbsp

1 Peel and remove the white skins of each fruit. Separate by cutting the segments of each fruit, collecting the juice in the same bowl.

2 Wash the spinach leaves, removing the stems. Drain well. Wash and drain lettuce leaves and bean sprouts. Pat the leaves dry in a cloth.

3 Arrange a bed of leaves on four plates. Place the mixture of citrus fruits in the centre with the juice. Decorate with red cherries and sprinkle over the peanuts. Drizzle a little oil over the leaves, then add seasoning.

Févettes à la Chinoise

Serves 4
Preparation 10 minutes
Cooking time 8 minutes

The skin of broad beans is tough yet edible. But when this tough membrane has been removed the green bean has a very delicate texture which in many ways has an affinity with pistachio nuts. In making this salad concoction, which I served to Royalties during my long career, I have found the secrets of flavour transfer as you can see in this recipe. Rich in protein and so delicate in taste.

	Metric	Imperial	American
Shelled broad (lima) beans	225 g	8 oz	8 oz
Pistachio nuts	50 g	2 oz	½ cup
Single (light) cream	75 ml	3 fl oz	6 tbsp
Drops of pistachio essence or 15 ml/1 tbsp Anisette liquor	6	6	6
Juice of lemon	1	1	1
Salt and pepper			
Chinese leaves	4	4	4
Large strawberries, sliced	8	8	8

1 Boil the broad beans for 7 minutes and drain. Remove the tough skin of each bean to reveal the green inner bean.

2 Scald the pistachio nuts and likewise remove the skin to reveal the green nut.

3 Combine the cream, essence or liquor and lemon juice in a bowl. Season with salt and pepper and toss the beans and nuts in this dressing.

4 Arrange one large Chinese leaf on each of the four plates. Spoon the bean mixture onto each leaf and garnish with slices of fresh strawberry.

Pickled Cauliflower Salad

Serves 4
Preparation 8 minutes
Cooking time 3 minutes,
plus marinating overnight.

The ubiquitous cauliflower of grandma's cheese cookery is often by-passed as an ingredient for salads. In salad-making this important vegetable can be eaten almost raw, as a pickle, in fact. It harmonizes well with eggs as in this recipe.

	Metric	Imperial	American
Small cauliflower	1	1	1
Salt			
Small gherkins (dill pickles)	12	12	12
Small pickling onions, peeled	12	12	12

	Metric	Imperial	American
Pickling sauce			
Dry white wine	150 ml	¼ pt	⅔ cup
Olive oil	3 tbsp	3 tbsp	3 tbsp
Wine vinegar	5 tbsp	5 tbsp	5 tbsp
Honey	2 tbsp	2 tbsp	2 tbsp
Coriander seeds	1 tsp	1 tsp	1 tsp
Black peppercorns	1 tsp	1 tsp	1 tsp
Salt	2 tsp	2 tsp	2 tsp
Turmeric	1 tsp	1 tsp	1 tsp
Green chilli, sliced	1	1	1
Iceberg lettuce, shredded	1	1	1
Celery seeds	1 tsp	1 tsp	1 tsp
Garnish			
Hard-boiled eggs	4	4	4

1 Separate the sprigs of a small cauliflower. Wash well and drain. Place in a large earthernware bowl or shallow dish.

2 Rub the gherkins with salt. Leave for 30 minutes, then wash off the salt, pat dry and place them in the dish with the cauliflower and onions.

3 In a pan, boil the wine, oil, vinegar, honey with all the seasonings and spices for 3 minutes. Pour the hot mixture over the raw vegetables. Leave to marinate overnight.

4 To serve, arrange a bed of shredded Iceberg lettuce on four plates and divide the mixture of pickled cauliflower sprigs. Drizzle a little of the pickling mixture over the salad. Garnish each plate with hard-boiled eggs, sliced neatly.

Hot Mushroom Salad

Serves 4
Preparation 8 minutes
Cooking time 2-3 minutes

This is one of the most popular type of modern salads. Any kind of mushrooms can be tossed in the pan and in a fraction of a second you have a tasty dish. Fresh field mushrooms are better than cultivated varieties for flavour and taste. As mushrooms will invariably pick up any other flavours such as garlic, onions or spices, this can be turned to advantage in salad-making of this kind.

	Metric	Imperial	American
Field mushrooms	225 g	8 oz	2 cups
Olive oil	4 tbsp	4 tbsp	4 tbsp
Small sprig of thyme	1	1	1
Salt and black pepper			
Cloves of garlic, chopped	2	2	2
Small fried bread croûtons			
Wine vinegar	2 tbsp	2 tbsp	2 tbsp
A selection of salad leaves to serve			

1 Clean and trim the mushrooms. Wash and drain, then cut in thin slices or quarter.

2 Heat the oil in a wok and stir-fry the mushrooms and thyme for 1 minute only. Season to taste and add the garlic and fried croûtons. Toss for 30 seconds, then remove the thyme.

3 Serve the mushrooms on the salad leaves placed on four plates. Drizzle a little vinegar over the salad mixture just before serving.

Cucumber and Mint in Yoghurt Dressing

Serves 4
Preparation 8 minutes, plus standing time
No cooking

This is a refreshing Indian dish.

	Metric	Imperial	American
Cucumber, peeled and halved, seeded and sliced	1	1	1
Salt and white pepper			
Plain Greek yoghurt	150 ml	¼ pt	⅔ cup
Cloves of garlic, chopped	2	2	2
Small green chilli, seeded and chopped	1	1	1
Fresh mint leaves, chopped	8	8	8
Chinese leaves	4	4	4

1 Place the cucumber in a large bowl. Sprinkle with 1 tsp salt and leave for 15 minutes to remove the bitter juices. Drain well, then rinse off in cold water. Drain well. Pat dry on a cloth.

2 Blend the yoghurt, garlic, chilli and chopped mint together. Season to taste. Combine the cucumber and dressing.

3 Arrange one Chinese leaf on each of four plates and fill them with a spoonful of cucumber salad.

— CHAPTER FIVE —

Light Meals
or Starters

* * * * * * * * * * * * * * * * * * * *

Vegetable and cheese fritters are firm favourites as light
meals or appetizers for informal parties. The two main
coatings most commonly used are egg batter and crumbs
or pancake batter mixture. All vegetables to be made into
fritters benefit from being marinated in oil and lemon
juice with spices prior to frying.

Cream Cheese Bonne Bouche

Serves 4
Preparation 10 minutes
Cooking time 1 minute per batch

	Metric	Imperial	American
Cream cheese	450 g	1 lb	1 lb
Eggs, beaten	2	2	2
White breadcrumbs	100 g	4 oz	2 cups
Ground almonds	1 tbsp	1 tbsp	1 tbsp
Cloves of garlic, chopped	2	2	2
Chopped fresh parsley	3 tbsp	3 tbsp	3 tbsp
Salt and black pepper			
Seasoned flour	8 tbsp	8 tbsp	8 tbsp
Oil for frying			
Batter mixture			
Flour	100 g	4 oz	1 cup
Eggs, beaten	2	2	2
Milk	600 ml	1 pint	2½ cups

1 In a large mixing bowl, blend the cream cheese, eggs, crumbs, ground almonds, garlic and parsley. Season.

2 Divide the mixture into 24 small balls. Shape them by hand with flour.

3 Beat the flour and eggs together, then gradually blend in the milk until smooth. Heat the oil in a shallow pan and dip the cheese balls into the batter, draining the surplus batter against the side of the bowl. Shallow fry for 1 minute per batch until golden. Drain on absorbent paper and serve on cocktail sticks with pineapple cubes.

Courges aux Amandes

Serves 4
Preparation 10 minutes
Cooking time 6-8 minutes

Boiled marrow is not everyone's favourite vegetable. Understandably enough as marrow is 90 per cent water. Therefore boiling it is an absurdity as all its flavour is lost. In this recipe I demonstrate the value of cooking marrow in butter.

	Metric	Imperial	American
Fresh marrow	450 g	1 lb	1 lb
Seasoned flour	8 tbsp	8 tbsp	8 tbsp
Eggs, beaten	3	3	3
Chopped fresh tarragon	1 tbsp	1 tbsp	1 tbsp
Chopped fresh basil	1 tbsp	1 tbsp	1 tbsp
Grated rind of lemon	1	1	1
Green chilli, chopped	1	1	1
Salt and black pepper			
Butter and oil mixed	6 tbsp	6 tbsp	6 tbsp
Flaked almonds	4 tbsp	4 tbsp	4 tbsp

1 Peel the marrow and cut in half. Scoop out the seeds. Cut the pulp into 5 cm/2 inch squares. Coat each piece in seasoned flour.

2 Mix the beaten eggs with herbs, grated lemon rind, chopped chilli and seasoning.

3 It is better to cook the marrow in two batches using a large 23 cm/9 inch frying pan. Heat 3 tbsp of the butter and oil until foaming and shallow fry half the marrow pieces on both sides for 3-4 minutes, turning over from time to time. Repeat with the remaining marrow. Place on a shallow dish.

4 Toast the flaked almonds and sprinkle on top of the fried marrow. Serve with wedges of tomatoes and use ordinary mayonnaise as a dip for the tomatoes.

Note:

The marrow should be fresh and tender. If old, parboil the peeled pieces for 1 minute only. Drain and pat dry well before refrying. All members of the squash family including pumpkin, courgettes (zucchini) and cucumbers can be cooked in this way.

Jerusalem Artichoke Sauté

Serves 4
Preparation 5 minutes
Cooking time 4 minutes

This is a tuber vegetable in season by the end of October. It can be boiled like new potatoes but only for 8 minutes. It can be fried in butter, or coated first in crumbs or batter as described in previous recipes. But sautéed with banana, peanuts and onions, it is a dish to remember.

	Metric	Imperial	American
Jerusalem artichokes	450 g	1 lb	1 lb
Butter and oil, mixed	6 tbsp	6 tbsp	6 tbsp
Bananas, not too ripe, peeled and sliced slantwise	2	2	2
Medium onion, chopped	1	1	1
Peanuts	100 g	4 oz	1 cup
Salt and pepper			
Juice and grated rind of lime	1	1	1

Garnish
Lettuce leaves
Mustard and cress

Chopped fresh parsley	2 tbsp	2 tbsp	2 tbsp

1 Scrub the artichokes with a brush, then wash well. Slice or leave whole as preferred. Drain and pat dry.

2 Heat the butter and oil in a shallow pan and sauté the artichokes and bananas for 2-3 minutes, then add the onion, peanuts, lime rind and juice. Toss for 1 minute more. Season to taste.

3 Serve on plates lined with 4 lettuce leaves and mustard and cress. Garnish with parsley.

Courgette Swiss Rarebit

Serves 4
Preparation 10-15 minutes
Cooking time about 5 minutes

Rarebit variations are endless as they can be served with vegetables, topped with eggs and even with baked beans. In this recipe, the cheese mixture is made with both Gruyère and Cheddar cheese.

	Metric	Imperial	American
Gruyère cheese and mature Cheddar, grated and mixed	225 g	8 oz	2 cups
Medium dry white wine	150 ml	¼ pint	⅔ cup
Cloves of garlic, finely chopped	2	2	2
Pinch of cayenne or chilli pepper			
Egg yolks	2	2	2
Cornflour (cornstarch)	1 tsp	1 tsp	1 tsp
Single (light) cream	4 tbsp	4 tbsp	4 tbsp
Kirsch	2 tbsp	2 tbsp	2 tbsp

Garnish

	Metric	Imperial	American
Courgettes (zucchini)	2	2	2
Slices of bread, crusts removed, or use French bread, sliced, allowing 4 per portion	16	16	16
Grated Parmesan cheese	4 tbsp	4 tbsp	4 tbsp
Paprika	1 tbsp	1 tbsp	1 tbsp
Tomato wedges to garnish			

1 In a saucepan, boil the grated cheese in the white wine with the garlic until melted. Add a pinch of cayenne or chilli pepper.

2 In a cup, mix the egg yolks, cornflour and cream. Gradually add this mixture to the boiling cheese, stirring to blend to a thickish paste. Remove from the heat and add the Kirsch last. Cool the mixture completely for easier spreading.

3 Toast the bread and keep hot.

4 Cut the courgettes slantwise into thin slices. Blanch for 30 seconds in boiling salted water. Drain and pat dry.

5 Spread the cheese mixture thickly onto the toast. Arrange overlapping slices of courgette on top. Sprinkle over grated Parmesan.

6 Place the rarebit on a baking tray and warm up under the grill (broiler) when ready to serve. Sprinkle on the paprika at the last moment. Top with a wedge of fresh tomato as a garnish.

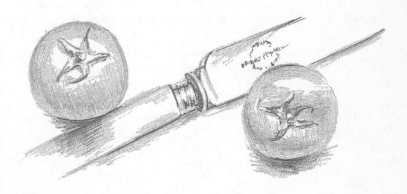

Tomato Piperade

Serves 4
Preparation 10-12 minutes
Cooking time 8 minutes

This is a mixture of scrambled eggs blended with fried peppers encased in a large tomato. As a stuffing this is a popular dish of the Basque region. To hold the tomato in shape, it is best to place it in an earthenware ramekin, 225 ml/8 fl oz/1 cup capacity.

	Metric	Imperial	American
Large tomatoes, 100 g/4 oz each	4	4	4

Filling

	Metric	Imperial	American
Oil	2 tbsp	2 tbsp	2 tbsp
Red pepper, split, seeded and chopped	1	1	1
Cloves of garlic, chopped	2	2	2
Large eggs, size 1 or 2	3	3	3
Double (heavy) cream	3 tbsp	3 tbsp	3 tbsp
Salt and pepper			
Chopped fresh parsley	2 tbsp	2 tbsp	2 tbsp

1 Cut the top off each tomato opposite the 'eye', two thirds from the top. Keep the slice as a hat. Squeeze out the seeds gently, scoop out the pulp and chop.

2 Heat the oil in a saucepan and stir fry the chopped pepper for 2 minutes, then add the garlic and chopped tomato pulp. Cook for 30 seconds more.

3 Blend half the beaten egg with the cream and add to the hot pepper mixture. Scramble for 1 minute, stirring, until smooth and cooked. Remove from the heat. Season and cool. Blend in remaining beaten egg to complete setting.

4 Fill the cavity of each tomato with this mixture. Place each tomato in a ramekin dish — this will prevent them from collapsing on baking.

5 Bake in a preheated oven at 200°C/400°F/gas mark 6 for 8 minutes. Replace the raw tomato slice on top of the cooked tomato. Sprinkle parsley on top and serve in the same ramekin dish.

Onion stuffed with Mushrooms and Olives

Serves 4
Preparation 15 minutes
Cooking time 30 minutes

Stuffed onions are very popular as a course on their own. The large sweet varieties are best for this kind of preparation.

	Metric	Imperial	American
Large onions, 100 g/4 oz each	4	4	4
Stock cube	1	1	1

	Metric	Imperial	American
Stuffing			
Butter	4 tbsp	4 tbsp	4 tbsp
Black olives, stoned (pitted)	12	12	12
Medium mushrooms, trimmed and chopped	4	4	4
Peanuts, chopped	6	6	6
Hard-boiled egg, chopped	1	1	1
Breadcrumbs	3 tbsp	3 tbsp	3 tbsp
Cloves of garlic, chopped	2	2	2
Chopped fresh basil	2 tbsp	2 tbsp	2 tbsp
Salt and pepper			
Egg, beaten	1	1	1
Grated Cheddar cheese	2 tbsp	2 tbsp	2 tbsp

1 Peel the onions, cut a slice off the top near the stem. Boil for 15 minutes. By squeezing, scoop out most of the inside, leaving a thick shell 1 cm/½ inch thick. Chop the centre part of the onion, leaving the four onions as cases for the filling.

2 For the stuffing, heat the butter and stir fry all the stuffing ingredients, except the egg and cheese. Mince them to a paste. In a bowl combine the ingredients with the egg. Season to taste.

3 Spoon the mixture into the onion cavities. Set them in individual ramekin dishes, 225 ml/8 fl oz/1 cup capacity. Boil ½ cup of water with 1 stock cube. Add this liquid to the onions from time to time as it evaporates during cooking. Cover with a lid and braise in a preheated oven at 190°C/375°F/gas mark 5 for 15 minutes. When nearly cooked, sprinkle with grated cheese and glaze under the grill (broiler).

Baked Timbale d'Aubergine

Serves 4
Preparation 10 minutes, plus standing time
Cooking time 20 minutes

This delicate aubergine dish is baked like a custard and served with a hot tomato coulis.

	Metric	Imperial	American
Aubergine (egg plant)	1	1	1
Salt and pepper			
Seasoned flour			
Oil	6 tbsp	6 tbsp	6 tbsp
Eggs, beaten	3	3	3
Single (light) cream	150 ml	¼ pint	⅔ cup
Clove of garlic, chopped	1	1	1
Tomato Coulis			
Tomatoes, seeded, skinned and finely chopped	4	4	4
Small red chilli, seeded and chopped	½	½	½
Cornflour (cornstarch) blended with 3 tbsp water	1 tsp	1 tsp	1 tsp
Salt	½ tsp	½ tsp	½ tsp
Sugar	½ tsp	½ tsp	½ tsp
Mint leaves	8	8	8

1 Peel and cut the aubergine into cubes. Sprinkle with salt and leave for 30 minutes to release the bitter juices. Wash and pat dry.

2 Coat the cubes in seasoned flour. Heat the oil and fry the aubergines for 1 minute. Drain on absorbent paper.

3 In a bowl, beat the eggs and cream together. Add the chopped garlic and seasoning. Half fill four ramekin dishes, capacity 200 ml/7 fl oz/1 cup each, with the cream mixture and top up with cooked aubergine. Place the ramekins in a deep tray half filled with hot water in the oven. Bake at 180°C/350°F/gas mark 4 for 15-20 minutes.

4 Meanwhile prepare the tomato coulis. Heat the tomato pulp and chopped chilli in a saucepan. Mix the cornflour and water in a cup and add to the tomato coulis. Cook for 4 minutes. Season with salt and sugar only.

5 To serve, pour a pool of the sauce onto four plates and turn out a custard onto each of them. Garnish with mint leaves.

Broccoli Beignets

Serves 4
Preparation 10 minutes
Cooking time 2-3 minutes

	Metric	Imperial	American
Broccoli, divided into 8 small sprigs	450 g	1 lb	1 lb
Marinade			
Juice of lemon	1	1	1
Oil	6 tbsp	6 tbsp	6 tbsp
Clove of garlic	1	1	1
Coarsely crushed black peppercorns and mustard seeds	1 tsp	1 tsp	1 tsp
Coating			
Seasoned flour	4 tbsp	4 tbsp	4 tbsp
Eggs, beaten with 3 tbsp water	3	3	3
Crumb mixture			
Breadcrumbs	2 tbsp	2 tbsp	2 tbsp
Cornmeal	2 tbsp	2 tbsp	2 tbsp
Chopped fresh parsley	2 tbsp	2 tbsp	2 tbsp
Oil for deep frying			

1 Liquidize the marinade ingredients and place in an earthernware dish.

2 Wash the broccoli sprigs and drain. Soak in the marinade for 15 minutes, turning over from time to time.

3 Heat the oil for deep frying to smoking point, 190°C/ 375°F. Have ready three soup plates, one with seasoned flour, one with beaten eggs and one with crumbs, corn-meal and chopped parsley well mixed together. Dip the broccoli sprigs in seasoned flour, then in beaten egg and finally well coat in crumb mixture.

4 Fry for 2-3 minutes. It is not necessary to cook the broccoli sprigs through as it is better to have them crunchy. Drain well on absorbent paper and serve hot with Tomato Barbecue sauce or curry sauce.

Variation
Cauliflower sprigs and small blanched sprouts can be cooked in the same way.

Tartlets de Petits Pois et Fromage Purée

Serves 4
Preparation 12 minutes plus standing time
Cooking time 15-20 minutes

In this flaky cheese pastry tartlet recipe the purée of peas has been blended with a light curd cheese, adding more food value in the process.

	Metric	Imperial	American
Made puff pastry	225 g	8 oz	8 oz
Cheddar cheese, grated	50 g	2 oz	½ cup
Chilli pepper	¼ tsp	¼ tsp	¼ tsp

	Metric	Imperial	American
Filling			
Cooked pea purée	125 g	5 oz	⅔ cup
Curd cheese, well drained	75 g	3 oz	6 tbsp
Shallot, chopped and fried for 30 seconds	1	1	1
Egg, beaten	1	1	1
Salt and pepper			
Honey	1 tsp	1 tsp	1 tsp

Garnish

Wedges of apple

1 On a floured board, roll out the pastry to 4 mm/ ⅙ inch thick.

2 Sprinkle over the grated cheese and chilli pepper and roll over to incorporate the cheese into the pastry. Prick the pastry with a fork to prevent rising. Cut out 8 rounds of pastry with a 6 cm/2½ inch pastry cutter. Grease the tins and line them with the pastry rounds. Prick the bottom of the pastry again. Rest for 20 minutes at kitchen temperature.

3 For the filling, blend the mashed peas, curd cheese, shallot and beaten egg in a bowl. Season with salt, honey and black pepper. Spoon the mixture into each tartlet. Smooth the top with a palette knife.

4 Bake in a preheated oven at 200°C/400°F/gas mark 6 for 15-20 minutes. Unmould onto a plate garnished with wedges of apples.

Caponata à la Conil

Serves 6
Preparation 10 minutes, plus standing time
Cooking time 30 minutes

So much has been said about our French ratatouille, often cooked to death so that all the good flavour is lost. A shorter cooking time is far better and this little vegetable stew becomes a party dish as popular as any cheese fondue. Okra pods are very gelatinous, giving more body to the sauce. They are available in supermarkets and Asian stores.

	Metric	Imperial	American
Aubergine (egg plant)	1	1	1
Salt and pepper			
Courgette (zucchini)	1	1	1
Red pepper	1	1	1
Olive oil	3 tbsp	3 tbsp	3 tbsp
Okra pods (Ladies' fingers), trimmed, stems removed	6	6	6
Medium onion, chopped	1	1	1
Large tomato, skinned, seeded and chopped	1	1	1
Medium sherry	150 ml	¼ pint	⅔ cup
Cloves of garlic, chopped	2	2	2
Basil	2 tbsp	2 tbsp	2 tbsp
Breadcrumbs	4 tbsp	4 tbsp	4 tbsp
Grated hard cheese	4 tbsp	4 tbsp	4 tbsp

1 Cut the aubergine into 2.5 cm/1 inch cubes. Sprinkle with salt and leave for 30 minutes to eliminate bitter juices. Wash, drain and pat dry.

2 Cut the courgette into wedges, then into cubes.

3 Cut the pepper in two lengthwise. Expose the shiny part on top and grill (broil) until it blisters. Peel the grilled skin. Cut the peeled part into small cubes.

4 Heat the oil in a pan and stir fry the vegetables, except the tomato, for 3 minutes. Then add tomato pulp, sherry, garlic and basil. Stew for 15 minutes only. Season to taste.

5 Divide the mixture into individual earthenware dishes, 225 ml/8 fl oz/1 cup capacity. Sprinkle over the breadcrumbs and grated cheese. Bake in a preheated oven at 200°C/400°F/gas mark 6 for 15 minutes to brown the top. Serve piping hot.

Sesame Cheesecake

Serves 6
Preparation 15 minutes
Cooking time 30 minutes

Savoury cheesecakes are as appreciated as the sweeter version. It is amazing what a little onion and chive can do to make more of a main dish or party snack.

	Metric	Imperial	American
Oil	4 tbsp	4 tbsp	4 tbsp
Large onion, sliced	1	1	1
Cream cheese	225 g	8 oz	1 cup
Blue cheese, mashed	50 g	2 oz	½ cup
Flour	1 tbsp	1 tbsp	1 tbsp
Eggs	3	3	3
Salt and black pepper			
Celery seeds	1 tbsp	1 tbsp	1 tbsp
Snipped chives			
Shortcrust pastry (basic pie dough)	225 g	8 oz	8 oz
Cheese, grated	50 g	2 oz	½ cup
Curry powder	2 tbsp	2 tbsp	2 tbsp
Pinch of sugar and salt			
Sesame seeds, separated	2 tbsp	2 tbsp	2 tbsp
Tomato and cucumber salad to garnish			

1 Heat the oil in a pan and stir fry the onion until soft, but not brown. Remove from the heat and cool.

2 In a bowl, mash the cream cheese and blue cheese together. Add the onion, flour and 3 egg yolks. Season with salt, pepper, celery seeds and chives. Leave aside for a moment.

3 Oil a 20 cm/8 inch cheesecake tin, 5 cm/2 inches deep with a removable bottom.

4 Roll out the pastry on a floured board to 4 mm/⅙ inch thick. Sprinkle over the grated cheese and curry powder, rolling the pastry to incorporate the powder as you dust it with flour. Cut a round of pastry to fit the bottom only of the cake tin. Line the tin with the round of pastry.

5 Knead the remaining pastry into a ball. Roll out to a strip 5 cm/2 inches wide as long as you have pastry left. Roll up this band of pastry and unroll it inside the tin, applying it with pressure against the side of the tin – this is the best way to line the side of a cheesecake. Seal to the base by brushing the corners with water.

6 Now beat the egg whites in a clean bowl until stiff and add a pinch of salt and sugar. Fold this mixture into the cheese preparation, then use to fill the tin. Sprinkle over sesame seeds. Bake in a preheated oven at 200°C/400°F/ gas mark 6 for 30 minutes.

7 Remove from the tin and slip it onto a large round flat dish or plate. Cut into portions and serve hot with salad.

Carrot and Spinach Tofu Cakes

Serves 6
Preparation 10-15 minutes
Cooking time 15 minutes

	Metric	Imperial	American
Carrots, peeled	175 g	6 oz	6 oz
Firm tofu	450 g	1 lb	1 lb
Flour, divided into 2 parts	75 g	3 oz	¾ cup
Grated nutmeg	1 tsp	1 tsp	1 tsp
Salt	1 tsp	1 tsp	1 tsp
Black pepper			
Spinach, cooked	275 g	10 oz	1½ cups
Eggs, beaten	2	2	2
Breadcrumbs or chopped nuts	225 g	8 oz	2 cups
Plum tomatoes, skinned and seeded	450 g	1 lb	1 lb
Soya sauce	1 tbsp	1 tbsp	1 tbsp
Malt vinegar	1 tbsp	1 tbsp	1 tbsp
Brown sugar	1 tbsp	1 tbsp	1 tbsp
Chilli pepper to taste			
Baby carrots, lightly cooked	350 g	12 oz	12 oz
Oil for frying			

1 Boil the carrots for 12-15 minutes. Drain and mash to a purée. Blend with half of the firm tofu and half of the flour to form a stiff paste.

2 Squeeze the cooked spinach as dry as possible, then blend with the remaining tofu anf flour to form a stiff paste. Season with nutmeg, salt and black pepper.

3 Shape the purée to a ball as big as an egg. Place two balls together and shape like a scone or cake. Freeze each cake to harden.

4 When hard, dip in seasoned flour, then beaten eggs and coat in breadcrumbs.

5 Liquidize the tomato to a coulis, add soya sauce, vinegar and sugar and a little salt and chilli pepper. Boil for 5 minutes and keep hot.

6 Heat oil in a shallow pan and deep fry the carrot cakes until golden for 1 minute. Fry no more than four at a time. Drain well.

7 Serve one cake per portion with baby boiled carrots and a spoonful of tomato sauce.

Chinese Cocktail Rolls

Serves 4
Preparation 8 minutes
Cooking time 5 minutes

This fried starter is very popular at cocktail parties.

	Metric	Imperial	American
Wonton pastry			
Flour	225 g	8 oz	2 cups
Salt and cayenne pepper			
Egg, beaten	1	1	1
Oil	2 tbsp	2 tbsp	2 tbsp
Filling			
Blue cheese	25 g	1 oz	¼ cup
Cream cheese	100 g	4 oz	½ cup
Chopped fresh parsley	2 tbsp	2 tbsp	2 tbsp
Chopped chives	2 tbsp	2 tbsp	2 tbsp
Salt and black pepper			
Field mushrooms, chopped	100 g	4 oz	1 cup
Egg, beaten	1	1	1
Breadcrumbs	2 tbsp	2 tbsp	2 tbsp
Peanuts, chopped	2 tbsp	2 tbsp	2 tbsp
Celery seeds	1 tsp	1 tsp	1 tsp
Oil for deep frying			
Coating			
Seasoned flour	2 tbsp	2 tbsp	2 tbsp
Eggs, beaten	2	2	2
Sesame seeds	2 tbsp	2 tbsp	2 tbsp

1 In a bowl, combine the flour, salt and pepper. Blend with the egg and oil to form a dough. Knead well, then leave to rest for 20 minutes, covered with a cloth.

2 Mix all the filling ingredients to a smooth paste. Divide into balls, then roll to 6 cm/2½ inch lengths, 2.5 cm/1 inch in diameter.

3 On a floured surface, roll out the pastry to 4 mm/⅙ inch thickness. Cut the pastry into rectangles 7.5×2.5 cm/3×1 inch.

4 Place a cheese roll inside each rectangle of pastry. Moisten the edges and roll up. Tuck the ends under and tightly roll each piece in flour. Dip in beaten egg, then coat with sesame seeds.

5 Heat oil in a pan and fry for 2 minutes until golden. Drain on absorbent paper and serve hot with tomato ketchup or other spicy sauces.

Pan Fried Asparagus and Egg Cutlets

Serves 4
Preparation 15 minutes, plus chilling
Cooking time 6-8 minutes

This is one of the most delicious hot starters with which to begin a celebration meal. Very good for a wedding reception. Use a well oiled shallow tray to cool the cutlet mixture.

	Metric	Imperial	American
Butter	50 g	2 oz	¼ cup
Flour	50 g	2 oz	½ cup
Milk	600 ml	1 pint	2½ cups
Eggs, beaten	2	2	2
Salt and pepper			
Grated nutmeg			
Oil for shallow frying			
Filling			
Asparagus tips	8	8	8
Eggs, hard-boiled and sliced	4	4	4

	Metric	Imperial	American
Coating			
Seasoned flour	4 tbsp	4 tbsp	4 tbsp
Eggs, beaten	2	2	2
Flaked almonds and cornflakes, crushed	100 g	4 oz	1 cup

1 To prepare a thick Béchamel sauce, heat the butter, add the flour and cook until smooth, without colouring. Gradually stir in the milk. When thick, remove from the heat and blend in the beaten eggs. Season with 1 tsp salt, ¼ tsp white pepper and a pinch of nutmeg.

2 Boil the asparagus for 5 minutes. Drain and cut into small pieces. Add them with the hard-boiled eggs to the sauce while still hot. Pour this mixture into a well-oiled shallow tray, 2.5 cm/1 inch deep. Chill until very cold.

3 Turn out the mixture onto a clean board and cut into squares. Coat each square with seasoned flour, dip in beaten eggs, then coat on both sides in crushed nuts and cornflakes.

4 Heat the oil until very hot and deep fry the squares for 1 minute on each side until golden. Do not fry more than four at a time. Drain on absorbent paper. Garnish with watercress or curly endive salad.

CHAPTER SIX

Pasta and Rice Dishes

* * * * * * * * * * * * * * * * * * * *

It may be easy to make noodles yourself, but with the range of egg pasta of every shape and size available in the shops, there is little need. The protein in flour, egg, cheese and other additional ingredients contributes to the nutritive value of pasta in a vegetarian diet. There are many ways of cooking pasta. Properly cooked pasta should be slightly crunchy or soft according to taste. Allow 50 g/2 oz uncooked pasta per person, which will swell to two and half times its original volume after cooking. Pasta can be served as an accompaniment for hot or cold salad dishes or on its own as a starter or main course.

Coquillettes aux Fèves

Serves 4
Preparation 10 minutes
Cooking time 10 minutes

	Metric	Imperial	American
Medium shell pasta	225 g	8 oz	8 oz
Broad (lima) beans	150 g	5 oz	1 cup
Sauce			
Butter	4 tbsp	4 tbsp	4 tbsp
Single (light) cream	150 ml	¼ pint	⅔ cup
Salt and pepper			
Grated nutmeg			
Chopped fresh parsley	2 tbsp	2 tbsp	2 tbsp

1 Boil the shell pasta in salted water for 8 minutes. Drain.

2 Boil the broad beans, then remove the outer skins.

3 In a wok or shallow pan, heat the butter and toss the pasta shells and beans for 1 minute. Add the cream, bring to the boil and season to taste, adding grated nutmeg. Sprinkle with parsley on serving.

Lasagna Verdi aux Aubergines

Serves 4
Preparation 15 minutes
Cooking time 15 minutes

This kind of pasta is sold in oblong pieces 6×15 cm/ 2½×6 inches. As the sheets tend to stick if cooked in a saucepan because of their size, it is best to boil them in a shallow roasting tray on top of the cooker with 2 tbsp oil added to the water. They will then be easy to separate. Usually this large pasta is baked in a large dish which is not as attractive as serving it in individual portions as in this recipe.

	Metric	Imperial	American
Lasagna pasta, 8 sheets	225 g	8 oz	8 oz
Filling			
Aubergine (egg plant)	1	1	1
Oil for frying			
Seasoned flour			
Spinach, stalks removed, washed, drained and dried	150 g	5 oz	5 oz
Butter	2 tbsp	2 tbsp	2 tbsp
Cloves of garlic, chopped	2	2	2
Mozzarella cheese	100 g	4 oz	4 oz
Salt and pepper			
Grated nutmeg			
Grated Parmesan and Cheddar cheese	3 tbsp	3 tbsp	3 tbsp

103

1 Place water and salt in a shallow tray and bring it to the boil. Cook the lasagna for 8 minutes. Remove, drain and pat dry on a clean cloth. Remove the sheets with a slicer without breaking them.

2 Cut the aubergines lenghthwise, 4 mm/⅙ inch thick. Sprinkle with salt and leave for 30 minutes. Then rinse and pat dry.

3 Heat 2 tbsp oil, dip each aubergine slice in flour, then fry for 1 minute only. Drain on absorbent paper. In the pan, heat 2 tbsp oil and cook the spinach for 5 minutes. Drain well and press to remove excess moisture.

4 Now take four individual oblong dishes, the kind used for hors d'oeuvres, and coat with butter, then sprinkle a little garlic on each one. Place one lasagna sheet, then an aubergine slice, topped with a slice of Mozzarella cheese and a layer of spinach on each dish. Season to taste with salt, pepper and grated nutmeg. Cover the spinach with another sheet of pasta, like a sandwich.

5 Brush the top with butter and sprinkle over mixture of grated Cheddar and Parmesan cheese. Bake in a pre-heated oven at 200°C/400°F/gas mark 6 for 8 minutes to glaze the top.

Spaghetti Romana New Style

Serves 4
Preparation 8 minutes
Cooking time 10 minutes

	Metric	Imperial	American
Thin spaghetti	225 g	8 oz	8 oz
Melted butter and oil	4 tbsp	4 tbsp	4 tbsp
White mushrooms, sliced	100 g	4 oz	1 cup
Cloves of garlic, chopped	2	2	2
Black (ripe) olives, stoned (pitted)	12	12	12
Pickled capers	1 tbsp	1 tbsp	1 tbsp
Green chilli, seeded and sliced	1	1	1
Large tomatoes, skinned seeded and sliced	4	4	4
Salt and pepper			
Ground mace			
Chopped fresh parsley and basil	2 tbsp	2 tbsp	2 tbsp
Grated Parmesan cheese			

1 Boil the spaghetti for 8 minutes until al dente. Drain.

2 In a wok, heat the butter and oil and toss the mushrooms, garlic, olives, capers and chilli for 1 minute. Reheat the spaghetti in this mixture for 1 minute more.

3 Add the tomatoes and toss several times. Season to taste. Sprinkle over the herbs, then serve on soup plates with grated Parmesan.

Polenta Gnocchi with Walnuts

Serves 4
Preparation 10 minutes
Cooking time 12 minutes

Most Latin countries produce their own version of cornmeal gnocchi. It is extremely nourishing and, when
enriched with egg and butter, the corn becomes alive.

	Metric	Imperial	American
Milk and water mixed	600 ml	1 pint	2½ cups
Sachet of saffron	1	1	1
Medium fine cornmeal	75 g	3 oz	⅔ cup
Egg yolks	2	2	2
Egg, beaten	1	1	1
Salt and black pepper			
Butter	50 g	2 oz	¼ cup
Oil and butter for frying gnocchi.			
Garnish			
Apples, cored and sliced	2	2	2
Walnuts	50 g	2 oz	½ cup
Seedless raisins	2 tbsp	2 tbsp	2 tbsp
Madeira wine	5 tbsp	5 tbsp	5 tbsp

1 Bring the milk and water to the boil, add saffron and sprinkle over the cornmeal, stirring. Boil for 6-8 minutes until thickened. Remove from the heat and add egg yolks, beaten egg, salt, pepper and butter.

2 Pour the hot mixture onto a buttered metal dish and spread it evenly. Allow to cool. When cold, turn the cold mixture onto a clean board. Cut in small 4 cm/1½ inch oblongs.

3 In a saucepan, heat oil and toss the apple slices, walnuts and seedless raisins for 2 minutes. Add the Madeira wine and boil for 1 minute.

4 Heat the oil and butter and refry the gnocchi until golden. Allow four per portion and serve on a plate with the apple and raisins in Madeira wine.

Ravioli alla Pope

Serves 4
Preparation 30 minutes, plus drying and poaching
Cooking time 15 minutes

	Metric	Imperial	American
Ravioli paste			
Strong bread flour	225 g	8 oz	2 cups
Salt	½ tsp	½ tsp	½ tsp
Large egg, size 1 or 2	1	1	1
Olive oil	1 tsp	1 tsp	1 tsp
Filling			
Oil	2 tbsp	2 tbsp	2 tbsp
Field mushrooms, finely chopped	100 g	4 oz	1 cup
Small onion, chopped	1	1	1
Clove of garlic, chopped	1	1	1
Tomato purée	1 tsp	1 tsp	1 tsp
Chopped fresh parsley	4 tbsp	4 tbsp	4 tbsp
Basil	4 tbsp	4 tbsp	4 tbsp
Flour	1 tbsp	1 tbsp	1 tbsp
Egg, beaten	1	1	1
Cream cheese	3 tbsp	3 tbsp	3 tbsp
Grated Parmesan			
Salt and black pepper			
Ground mace			
Semolina to sprinkle			

1 Mix the flour and salt in a bowl. Make a hollow in the flour and add the egg, oil and 1 tsp water. Mix to a dough and knead on a floured board for 8 minutes. Cover with an inverted bowl and rest for 1 hour.

2 In a wok, heat the oil and stir fry the mushrooms, onion and garlic for 3 minutes. Add the tomato purée, parsley, basil, 1 tbsp flour and beaten egg, stirring briskly. Remove from the heat and blend in the cream cheese and Parmesan. Season to taste.

3 To fill the ravioli, roll out the pastry to 3 mm/⅛ inch thick, on a floured board. Roll out the pastry to a square which can be folded in two. On one side of the square spoon some filling at regular intervals. Fold over the other side of the pastry. With a ruler, mark squared lines between each filling. Using a ravioli cutter, separate each square by indenting the cutter into the paste.

4 Sprinkle uncooked semolina over a tray lined with paper. Place the ravioli on the try and allow them to dry on the rack above the cooker or in a hot place for 2 hours.

5 To poach, boil in a shallow tray half filled with salted water for 8 minutes. Drain well. Coat with tomato sauce (page 32). (The ravioli will be more tender if marinated in a plain tomato sauce and left overnight to soak up the sauce.)

6 When needed, bake in individual dishes, four per portion. Sprinkle with grated cheese and bake at 200°C/400°F/gas mark 6 for 15 minutes.

Crépes aux Poireaux

Serves 4
Preparation 10-15 minutes
Cooking time 5-10 minutes

	Metric	Imperial	American
Leeks, white parts only	2	2	2
Butter	50 g	2 oz	¼ cup
Batter			
Self raising flour	100 g	4 oz	1 cup
Eggs, beaten	2	2	2
Beer and water in equal proportions	600 ml	1 pint	2½ cups
Salt			
Oil for cooking pancakes	5 tbsp	5 tbsp	5 tbsp
Filling			
Cream cheese	75 g	3 oz	6 tbsp
Dolcelatte blue cheese	75 g	3 oz	3 oz
Egg, beaten	1	1	1
Grated cheese	3 tbsp	3 tbsp	3 tbsp

1 Clean the leeks and cut the white part in thin slices. Wash, drain and pat dry. Heat the butter in a frying pan and shallow fry the leeks over a low heat for 2 minutes without browning until soft and cooked. Transfer the butter and leeks to a large bowl.

2 Blend the leeks with the flour, beaten eggs, beer and water to form a thin pancake batter. Season with a pinch of salt.

3 Heat oil in a small pancake pan and pour in 45 ml/ 3 tbsp of batter. Cook on both sides for 1 minute until golden. Turn onto a flat tray to cool. Make eight thin pancakes.

4 For the filling: in a bowl, cream the cheese and blue cheese with the beaten egg. Season to taste. Spread this mixture on one pancake and sandwich it with another to produce four portions.

5 Place the double pancakes on a large baking tray. Sprinkle with the grated cheese and glaze under the grill (broiler). Serve flat on a plate, cut in four triangular pieces.

Tarte de Champignons in Brandy Sauce

Serves 4
Preparation 10 minutes
Cooking time 20-30 minutes

For this recipe use a prebaked flan case or make your own.

	Metric	Imperial	American
Shortcrust pastry	225 g	8 oz	8 oz
Butter, melted	50 g	2 oz	¼ cup
Grated cheese	50 g	2 oz	½ cup
Filling			
Butter	50 g	2 oz	¼ cup
Button mushrooms, trimmed	450 g	1 lb	1 lb
Shallots, chopped	2	2	2
Salt and pepper			
Grated nutmeg			
Brandy	4 tbsp	4 tbsp	4 tbsp
Single (light) cream	150 ml	¼ pint	⅔ cup
Eggs, beaten	2	2	2

1 Roll out the pastry on a floured board to 4 mm/⅙ inch thick. Cut out a round to fit a flat tin, 23 cm/9 inches in diameter. Oil the tin and line it with the pastry. Brush with butter. Put in a piece of foil and fill with dry beans. Bake blind in a preheated oven at 200°C/400°F/gas mark 6 for 15 minutes. Remove the beans and foil.

2 For the filling: in a wok or pan, heat the butter and stir fry the mushrooms and shallots for 2 minutes. Season. Add the brandy and remove from the heat., In a cup, blend the eggs and cream.

3 Sprinkle the bottom of pastry case with grated cheese and add the mushrooms. Cover with the egg mixture. Bake in the oven for 12-15 minutes until the custard is set. Serve hot or cold.

Macédoine Flan

Serves 4
Preparation 12-15 minutes
Cooking time 25 minutes

This presentation of mixed vegetables with hard-boiled eggs in pastry can be eaten hot or cold.

	Metric	Imperial	American
Baked flan case, 23 cm/9 inch diameter	1	1	1
Filling			
Mixture of diced carrots, turnips, peas, beans, sweetcorn, chopped onions and baked beans, allowing about 25 g/1 oz of each	225 g	8 oz	8 oz
Grated cheese	50 g	2 oz	½ cup
Chopped fresh parsley	2 tbsp	2 tbsp	2 tbsp
Single (light) cream	150 ml	¼ pint	⅔ cup
Made mustard	1 tsp	1 tsp	1 tsp
Eggs, beaten	2	2	2
Salt and pepper			
Hard-boiled eggs, shelled and halved	4	4	4

1 Boil the vegetable mixture for 3 minutes only and drain well. Place in a bowl.

2 Brush the bottom of the pastry case with butter and sprinkle with the grated cheese and parsley.

3 In a cup, mix the cream, made mustard and beaten eggs. Season with salt and pepper. Blend this mixture with the vegetables.

4 Fill the flan case with the vegetables. Bake in a pre-heated oven at 200°C/400°F/gas mark 6 for 25 minutes. Cool. When cold divide into eight portions. Top each portion with half an egg. Serve with lettuce leaves.

Note:
For extra dry cheese, as good as Parmesan, simply freeze Cheddar or similar cheese unwrapped.

Pilaf with Saffron

Serves 4
Preparation 10 minutes
Cooking time 20 minutes

	Metric	Imperial	American
Oil	2 tbsp	2 tbsp	2 tbsp
Medium onion, chopped	1	1	1
Long grain rice	125 g	4½ oz	1 cup
Water	600 ml	1 pint	2½ cups
Yeast extract	1 tbsp	1 tbsp	1 tbsp
Sachet of saffron	1	1	1
Salt and black pepper			
Ground turmeric	1 tsp	1 tsp	1 tsp
Sweetcorn kernels	75 g	3 oz	¾ cup

1 In a shallow pan heat the oil and stir fry the onion for 1 minute. Add the rice to absorb the oil. Add the water and yeast extract and bring to the boil. Season to taste, including the saffron and turmeric. Add the sweetcorn and boil for 5 minutes.

2 Transfer the mixture into a pie dish. Cover with greased paper and bake in the oven at 200°/400°/gas mark 6 for 15 minutes.

3 To serve, oil a small metal tumbler. Fill it with rice and pack tightly turn onto a plate like a sandcastle. Serve the rice with a tomato coulis, see page 85, and grated cheese.

Pilaff aux Chataignes

Serves 4
Preparation 5 minutes, plus making pilaf
Cooking time 20 minutes

Chestnuts can be purchased in tins already boiled, or in dried form which needs soaking for 3 hours. Fresh chestnuts should be skinned twice. The hard skin is slit and baked in a very hot oven until it blisters then the nut must be boiled for 10 minutes to remove the soft skin. In this recipe the cooked chestnuts are added to the Pilaf with Saffron on page 116.

	Metric	Imperial	American
Cooked Pilaf with saffron	225 g	8 oz	8 oz
Fresh boiled chestnuts	150 g	5 oz	1 cup
Cheese, grated	50 g	2 oz	½ cup

1 Combine all ingredients and serve in individual dishes.

Spanish Paella

Serves 4
Preparation 10 minutes
Cooking time 30-40 minutes

	Metric	Imperial	American
Oil	3 tbsp	3 tbsp	3 tbsp
Medium onion, chopped	1	1	1
Long-grain rice	150 g	5 oz	1 cup
Ground turmeric	1 tsp	1 tsp	1 tsp
Curry powder	1 tsp	1 tsp	1 tsp
Salt to taste			
Green chilli, sliced	1	1	1
Red and green peppers, seeded and diced	75 g	3 oz	¾ cup
Garlic cloves, chopped	2	2	2
Green olives, stoned (pitted)	50 g	2 oz	½ cup
Tomatoes, skinned, seeded and chopped	2	2	2
Water	500 ml	¾ pint	2 cups
Vegetable stock (bouillon) cube	1	1	1
Pine kernels	50 g	2 oz	½ cup
Marrow peas	50 g	2 oz	½ cup

use peas or beans.

1 Place a 1.75 litre/3 pint/7½ cup metal paella pan on the stove and heat the oil. Stir fry the onion for 1 minute, then add the rice, turmeric, curry powder, salt, chilli, peppers, green olives, water and stock cube. Boil for 5 minutes. Add the tomatoes, pine kernels and peas.

2 Cover the paella and transfer to the oven preheated to 200°C/400°F/gas mark 6. Bake for 30-40 minutes.

Stuffed Peppers

Serves 4
Preparation 10 minutes, plus making paella
Cooking time 30 minutes

	Metric	Imperial	American
Red peppers	4	4	4
Eggs, beaten	2	2	2
Cold cooked Spanish paella	225 g	8 oz	8 oz

1 Cut the top with the stem still attached from the peppers and set aside. Make an opening in the pepper tops and remove the seeds with a spoon.

2 In a bowl, blend the eggs with the cooked paella. Spoon the mixture into the cavities of the peppers. Stand them in a deep earthenware dish. Part fill the dish with hot water and bake in the oven at 200°C/400°F/gas mark 6 for 30 minutes. Meanwhile blanch the pepper top stems and sit them on top of the cooked peppers.

cooked it for Lesley & Shlomo. Rice was nice but
let the peppers overcook unfortunately all ok.

Timbale de Riz Parisienne

Serves 6
Preparation 10 minutes
Cooking time 55-65 minutes

	Metric	Imperial	American
Short grain pudding rice	75 g	3 oz	½ cup
Milk, heated	600 ml	1 pint	2½ cups
Single (light) cream	100 ml	4 fl oz	½ cup
Egg yolks, beaten	3	3	3
Salt and pepper			
Grated nutmeg			
White mushrooms, sliced	100 g	4 oz	1 cup
Butter	50 g	2 oz	¼ cup

1 Place the rice in a deep ovenproof dish and cover with the milk. Bake in the oven at 180°C/350°F/gas mark 4 for 40-50 minutes. Cool completely.

2 In a bowl, mix the cream and egg yolks. Add the cooked rice. Season with salt, pepper, nutmeg and add the sliced mushrooms.

3 Butter six small metal tumbler moulds and fill them with the mixture. Place in deep tray half filled with hot water. Bake in the oven at 200°C/400°F/gas mark 6 for 15 minutes. Turn out onto six plates.

Wild Rice Lentil Casserole

Serves 4
Preparation 5 minutes
Cooking time 30 minutes

Wild 'rice' comes from a tall North American aquatic plant, Zizania aquatica. It can be bought loose and takes 55 minutes to cook. There is now a bought product available that mixes long grain and wild rice and takes only 20-30 minutes to cook. This is also cheaper than using wild rice on its own.

	Metric	Imperial	American
Long grain and wild rice mixture	150 g	5 oz	1 cup
Green lentils	100 g	4 oz	½ cup
Oil and butter	50 ml	2 fl oz	¼ cup
Medium onion, chopped	1	1	1
Medium carrot, diced	1	1	1
Tomato purée	1 tbsp	1 tbsp	1 tbsp
Salt and pepper			
Curry powder	1 tsp	1 tsp	1 tsp

1 Boil the rice and lentils separately for 20 minutes, then drain. Combine the rice and lentils.

2 In a wok, stir fry the onion and carrot for 3 minutes. Add the rice and lentils with the tomato purée and all the seasoning. Heat for 5 minutes.

3 Serve as stuffing for cooked pancakes, or spoon onto Chinese leaves.

Rice Cake

Serves 4
Preparation 10 minutes, plus making pilaf
Cooking time 5-10 minutes

	Metric	Imperial	American
Eggs, beaten	2	2	2
Cold Pilaf with saffron (see page 116)	225 g	8 oz	8 oz
Seasoned flour			
Eggs, beaten, for coating	2	2	2
Mixture of crumbs and fine cornmeal	50 g	2 oz	½ cup
Oil for shallow frying			

1 In a bowl, blend the 2 beaten eggs into cold cooked rice pilaf. Divide the mixture into four cakes or balls. Dip in seasoned flour, then in beaten eggs and lastly coat in crumb mixture.

2 Heat the oil in a shallow pan and fry the cakes for 2 minutes on each side until golden. Serve with green salad or cooked mangetout peas (snow peas).

Risotto Verde

Serves 4
Preparation 10 minutes
Cooking time 25-30 minutes

This risotto could be used as a filling for marrow, courgette, tomato or peppers. Or serve on its own sprinkled with grated cheese and accompanied with hard-boiled eggs and tomato salad.

	Metric	Imperial	American
Butter and oil	50 ml	2 fl oz	¼ cup
Small onion, chopped	1	1	1
Small grain Patna rice	150 g	5 oz	1 cup
Water	600 ml	1 pint	2½ cups
Vegetable stock cube	1	1	1
Fresh spinach, stalks removed, washed, drained and cut in shreds	150 g	6 oz	1 cup
Tarragon leaves, chopped	6	6	6
Salt and black pepper			
Single (light) cream	50 ml	2 fl oz	¼ cup
Grated Parmesan cheese	50 g	2 oz	½ cup

1 Heat the butter and oil in a sauté pan and stir fry the onion until soft but not brown. Add the rice and stir for 1 minute, then add the water and stock cube.

2 Boil for 15-20 minutes, then add the shredded spinach, tarragon and seasoning. Cook gently for another 5 minutes only.

3 Lastly blend in the cream, cheese and season to taste. The rice should be softer than for pilaf and more creamy.

Indian Kedgeree

Serves 4
Preparation 5 minutes, plus making pilaf
Cooking time 20 minutes

	Metric	Imperial	American
Cooked Pilaf with saffron (see page 116)	225 g	8 oz	8 oz
Curry powder	1 tbsp	1 tbsp	1 tbsp
Desiccated coconut	2 tbsp	2 tbsp	2 tbsp
Yoghurt	3 tbsp	3 tbsp	3 tbsp
Hard-boiled eggs, shelled and sliced	4	4	4

1 Prepare the rice pilaf and mix it with the curry powder and coconut.

2 When cooked, blend in the yoghurt and serve hot with sliced hard-boiled eggs.

Note:
The deficiency in vitamin B complex in polished rice can be supplemented by using yeast extracts but when items such as eggs, nuts and pulses are added to a dish this is not a problem. If preferred use brown rice and allow ten more minutes of cooking time.

French Pea Baguette Slice

Serves 4
Preparation 10 minutes
Cooking time 15 minutes

This is a delicious pizza kind of starter which is made with French bread toasted and coated with a creamy pea purée, bound with egg and cheese and glazed.

	Metric	Imperial	American
Long French bread, split and divided into 4 pieces	1	1	1
Butter	50 g	2 oz	¼ cup
Cloves of garlic, chopped	2	2	2
Chopped fresh parsley	2 tbsp	2 tbsp	2 tbsp
Dried thyme powder	1 tsp	1 tsp	1 tsp
Filling			
Fresh or processed peas	100 g	4 oz	1 cup
Egg, beaten	1	1	1
Double (heavy) cream	3 tbsp	3 tbsp	3 tbsp
Spring onion (scallion), chopped	25 g	1 oz	2 tbsp
Hard cheese, grated	100 g	4 oz	1 cup

1 Toast the four pieces of French bread.

2 Prepare a garlic paste by creaming the butter with the garlic, parsley and thyme. Spread this mixture onto the bread.

3 Boil the peas for 10 minutes, then mash to a purée. In a bowl, combine the peas purée with the beaten egg, cream and chopped onion.

4 Spread the mixture thickly over the bread. Sprinkle with grated cheese and glaze under the grill (broiler) until golden.

Note:
For a more attractive presentation, the bread can be cut into rounds, allowing three rounds per person.

Prime Pumpkin Pie

Serves 8
Preparation 10 minutes
Cooking time 40 minutes

Use a 20 cm/8 inch diameter, 5 cm/2½ inch deep cake ring tin on a baking sheet or tray, oiled and with the edges lined with a band of greaseproof paper, 6 cm/ 3 inches deep.

We now see ample supplies of pumpkins. Children may still like to use them at hallowe'en, but the real gourmets will make good soups and sweet flans and, in this instance, a savoury cheesecake.

	Metric	Imperial	American
Savoury pastry (see recipe page 138)	350 g	12 oz	12 oz

	Metric	Imperial	American
Filling			
Pumpkin, pulp only, cut into 2.5 cm/1 inch cubes.	225 g	8 oz	8 oz
Cream cheese	175 g	6 oz	¾ cup
Cooked rice	100 g	4 oz	⅔ cup
Egg whites, beaten to a meringue	2	2	2
Salt and pepper			
Ground ginger	¼ tsp	¼ tsp	¼ tsp
Tomato purée	15 g	½ oz	1 tbsp
Flour	25 g	1 oz	¼ cup
Salted peanuts	25 g	2 tbsp	2 tbsp

1 Line the ring tin with the pastry, 4 mm/⅙ inch thick.

2 Boil the pumpkin cubes in salted water for 10 minutes. Drain, then cool.

3 In a large bowl, blend the cream cheese, rice, egg white meringue, seasoning, tomato purée and flour. Add the pumpkin cubes and stir well.

4 Fill the pastry shell to the top. Sprinkle over the peanuts. Bake in the oven at 200°C/400°F/gas mark 6 for 30 minutes. Cool and serve cold with a tomato salad.

— CHAPTER SEVEN —

Egg Dishes

* *

Eggs are the cheapest and most nutritious food, available in large quantities in all western countries. A pity that the habit of eggs for breakfast has been replaced by cereals and the ubiquitous muesli mixture. Hundreds of egg recipes are available with numerous permutations for each basic dish. In this book we only suggest the use of free range eggs of the freshest quality.

Poached Egg Turkish Style

Serves 2
Preparation 5 minutes, plus standing
Cooking time 8 minutes

	Metric	Imperial	American
Yoghurt	100 ml	4 fl oz	½ cup
Juice of lemon	½	½	½
Clove of garlic, chopped	1	1	1
Butter	2 tbsp	2 tbsp	2 tbsp
Eggs	2	2	2

1 Blend the yoghurt, lemon juice and garlic in a bowl. Leave for 20 minutes, then strain.

2 Place a spoonful of the mixture into two buttered ramekin dishes and add an egg to each. Put the dishes in a deep tray half filled with water. Cover with foil.

3 Poach in the oven at 200°C/400°F/gas mark 6 for 8 minutes. Serve in the same dishes.

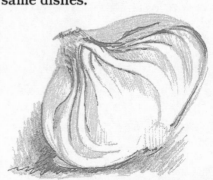

Shredded Omelette Japanese Style

Serves 2
Preparation 5-8 minutes
Cooking time 8 minutes

	Metric	Imperial	American
Eggs, beaten	4	4	4
Soya sauce	1 tbsp	1 tbsp	1 tbsp
Grated ginger	1 tsp	1 tsp	1 tsp
Salt and pepper			
Sugar	½ tsp	½ tsp	½ tsp
Snipped chives			
Oil for frying			
Shredded Iceberg lettuce			

1 In a bowl, beat the eggs and add the soya sauce, ginger, salt, pepper, sugar and chives.

2 Heat 1 tsp oil in an omelette pan. Pour in 50 ml/2 fl oz of egg mixture and cook like a pancake for 1 minute. Toss on other side and slip onto a tray. Continue until you have four omelettes. Put them on top of each other. Roll them and cut into shreds with a sharp knife. To serve, place shredded lettuce on four plates and top with the egg ribbons.

Italian Style Frittata

Serves 6
Preparation 10 minutes
Cooking time 5-8 minutes

	Metric	Imperial	American
Butter	2 tbsp	2 tbsp	2 tbsp
Leaf spinach stalks removed, washed and dried	450 g	1 lb	1 lb
Eggs, beaten	6	6	6
Single (light) cream	3 tbsp	3 tbsp	3 tbsp
Salt and pepper			
Grated nutmeg			
Clove of garlic, chopped	1	1	1
Oil and butter, mixed	4 tbsp	4 tbsp	4 tbsp
Grated Parmesan cheese	2 tbsp	2 tbsp	2 tbsp
Fontina cheese or semi soft cheese, cut into small cubes	25 g	1 oz	¼ cup
Walnuts, chopped	6	6	6

1 In a pan, melt the butter and cook the spinach for 5 minutes. Remove. Squeeze out surplus water to make it as dry as possible. Chop the cooked spinach.

2 Blend the beaten eggs with the spinach, cream and seasoning, including the chopped garlic.

3 In a shallow frying pan 20 cm/8 inches in diameter, heat the oil and butter until smoking. Stir in the egg mixture and scramble a little. Sprinkle with grated Parmesan cheese. Add the cubes of Fontina cheese and walnuts. Cook, without stirring, for 2 minutes, making sure the bottom does not stick to the pan.

4 When the underside is brown, place a cover or large plate over the omelette. Turn the pan upside down to turn frittata onto a plate. Slide it from the plate back into the pan, adding a little oil. Brown on other side for 1 minute. When ready, the frittata should be soft but set like a sponge cake. Serve on a large flat plate. Cut in wedges and serve with lettuce, tomatoes and French dressing.

Chinese Omelette

Serves 2
Preparation 5 minutes
Cooking time 6 minutes

	Metric	Imperial	American
Red peppers	75 g	3 oz	3 oz
Bean sprouts	100 g	4 oz	2 cups
Eggs, beaten	4	4	4
Soya sauce	1 tbsp	1 tbsp	1 tbsp
Salt and pepper			
Flour	½ tbsp	½ tbsp	½ tbsp
Chinese spice powder	½ tbsp	½ tbsp	½ tbsp
Oil	2 tbsp	2 tbsp	2 tbsp
Clove of garlic, chopped	1	1	1
Chopped ginger	1 tsp	1 tsp	1 tsp
Shredded Iceberg lettuce leaves			

1 Cut the red pepper into fine julienne matchsticks. Wash the bean sprouts and drain well.

2 In a bowl, beat the eggs and flavour with soya sauce, salt and pepper, flour and Chinese spices.

3 In a wok, heat the oil and stir fry the red pepper and sprouts for 2 minutes. Add the garlic and ginger and cook for 30 seconds.

4 Now stir in the beaten eggs, scrambling a little. Cook for 2 minutes, without browning, then toss or turn over like a pancake to cook on both sides. Slip onto a plate and serve on a bed of shredded lettuce.

Pain Perdu

Serves 8
Preparation 5 minutes
Cooking time 15 minutes

	Metric	Imperial	American
Eggs	4	4	4
Salt and pepper			
Sugar	½ tsp	½ tsp	½ tsp
Slices of bread, crusts removed	8	8	8
Oil and butter, mixed	4 tbsp	4 tbsp	4 tbsp

Garnish
Sliced tomatoes or
   fresh strawberries

1 Beat the eggs with the salt, pepper and sugar in a large shallow dish. Dip the bread slices in this mixture.

2 Heat the oil and butter in a large pan. Fry the soaked slices, one at a time for 1 minute on each side until golden. Drain on absorbent paper. Garnish with sliced tomatoes, or with fresh strawberries as a sweet.

French Asparagus Soufflé Omelette

Serves 1
Preparation 15 minutes
Cooking time about 10 minutes

For this omelette you need a small black iron pancake pan. Make sure it is clean and well oiled otherwise the omelette will stick to the pan. To make sure, heat 3 tbs of oil in the pan for 4 minutes then tip out the oil. Your pan has been conditioned.

	Metric	Imperial	American
Egg	1	1	1
Egg yolks	2	2	2
Egg whites	2	2	2
Salt and white pepper			
Lemon juice	½ tsp	½ tsp	½ tsp
Butter and oil	2 tbsp	2 tbsp	2 tbsp
Asparagus tips, fresh or canned	4	4	4
Little butter			

1 In a bowl, beat the whole egg with the egg yolks. Season.

2 In another bowl, free of grease, beat the egg whites with the lemon juice until meringue-like. Fold the meringue into the egg yolk mixture. Cook or heat the asparagus.

3 Heat the butter and oil in the conditioned pan and cook the egg mixture gently over low heat, without stirring. With a palette knife, lift the omelette to ensure it does not get too brown underneath. Cover with a lid and allow to puff up for 30 seconds.

4 At this stage, place the well drained hot asparagus in the middle of the omelette. Fold over. Slip the omelette carefully onto a flat ovenproof dish coated with butter. Bake in the oven at 200°C/400°F/gas mark 6 for 5-8 minutes to allow for more puffing. Serve.

Variation:
This omelette can be filled with strawberries or fried banana as a dessert, omitting the salt and pepper and using a little sugar instead.

Egg Bretonne

Serves 4
Preparation 5 minutes, plus making pancakes
Cooking time 8 minutes

	Metric	Imperial	American
Thin pancakes	4	4	4
Butter, softened	4 tbsp	4 tbsp	4 tbsp
Eggs	4	4	4

1 Place the pancakes onto a baking tray. Brush with butter.

2 Break an egg on each pancake. Cover with foil and bake in the oven at 220°C/425°F/gas mark 7 for 8 minutes.

Broccoli and Tomato Quiche

Serves 8
Preparation 20 minutes
Cooking time 35 minutes

	Metric	Imperial	American
Basic savoury pastry			
Plain (all-purpose) flour	225 g	8 oz	2 cups
Salt	½ tsp	½ tsp	½ tsp
Mustard powder	½ tsp	½ tsp	½ tsp
Margarine or butter	100 g	4 oz	½ cup
Large egg, size 1 or 2, beaten	1	1	1
Filling			
Broccoli florets, cut in small pieces	225 g	8 oz	8 oz
Tomatoes, skinned, seeded and coarsely chopped	150 g	6 oz	¾ cup
Cloves of garlic, chopped	2	2	2
Small onion, chopped	1	1	1
Salt and pepper			
Milk	300 ml	½ pint	1¼ cups
Eggs, beaten	3	3	3
Grated nutmeg	½ tsp	½ tsp	½ tsp
Cheddar cheese, grated	100 g	4 oz	1 cup

1 Rub the flour, salt and mustard powder together, then add the butter and blend to a crumble.

2 Stir in the egg and knead lightly. Roll into a ball and cover with a cloth and leave to rest in a cool place or a fridge until required.

3 Parboil the broccoli for 8 minutes. Drain and chop coarsely. Blend with the tomato pulp, onions and garlic. Season to taste.

4 In a bowl, combine the milk, beaten eggs and nutmeg.

5 Roll the pastry to 4 mm/⅙ inch thick. Line a well greased 20 cm/8 inch quiche tin.

6 Spoon the broccoli filling into the pastry case. Sprinkle the grated cheese on top and pour the egg mixture over.

7 Bake in the oven at 200°C/400°F/gas mark 6 for 35 minutes until set and golden.

Greek Cheese and Spinach Pie

Serves 8
Preparation 20 minutes, plus resting
Cooking time 30 minutes

	Metric	Imperial	American
Phyllo pastry or fatless dough			
Bread dough flour	450 g	1 lb	4 cups
Salt	1 tsp	1 tsp	1 tsp
Water	225 ml	8 fl oz	1 cup
Olive oil	2 tbsp	2 tbsp	2 tbsp
Filling			
Milk	600 ml	1 pint	2½ cups
Semolina	75 g	3 oz	½ cup
Cheddar cheese, grated	100 g	4 oz	1 cup
Cream cheese	100 g	4 oz	½ cup
Eggs, beaten	3	3	3
Oil or butter	2 tbsp	2 tbsp	2 tbsp
Leaf spinach, washed and trimmed	100 g	4 oz	4 oz
Cloves of garlic, chopped	2	2	2
Salt and black pepper			
Grated nutmeg	½ tsp	½ tsp	½ tsp
Sunflower oil	75 ml	3 fl oz	6 tbsp

1 Mix all the pastry ingredients together until a dough is formed. Leave to rest for 20 minutes.

2 In a large, heavy saucepan, bring the milk to the boil and sprinkle over the semolina. Cook for 5 minutes until thick, like porridge. Put the cooked semolina paste into a large mixing bowl. Blend in the cheeses and beaten eggs. Cool the mixture completely.

3 In a shallow pan, heat the oil and stir fry the spinach leaves and garlic for 5 minutes. Remove from the heat and chop the mixture coarsely. Blend it into the main mixture. Season to taste, adding the nutmeg.

4 Lay a clean cloth on a table and sprinkle with flour. Divide the phyllo paste into 50 g/2 oz balls. Roll out as thinly as possible, then stretch thinner by pulling it all round to paper thickness. Cut it into 12 sheets to fit a well oiled 30 cm/12 inch baking tin.

5 Place six sheets of the pastry as the base. Spread the filling over and cover with the remaining six sheets on top of each other, sprinkling melted butter or oil over. With the tip of a knife, mark criss cross lines to form a pattern. Bake in the oven at 200°C/400°F/gas mark 6 for 30 minutes, then cut along the marked lines.

Note:
Puff pastry can be used instead of filo but only 2 layers will be needed.

Tarte de Tomates et Haricots Verts Niçoise

Serves 6
Preparation 15 minutes
Cooking time 25 minutes

	Metric	Imperial	American
Puff pastry	225 g	8 oz	8 oz
Cheddar cheese, grated	50 g	2 oz	½ cup
Paprika	1 tsp	1 tsp	1 tsp
Oil	2 tbsp	2 tbsp	2 tbsp
Medium onion, chopped	75 g	3 oz	¾ cup
Clove of garlic, chopped	1	1	1
Tomatoes, skinned, seeded and coarsely chopped	4	4	4
Black olives, stoned (pitted)			
Lightly cooked French beans, cut into small cubes	75 g	3 oz	¾ cup
Salt and black pepper			
Ground mace			
Chopped fresh basil	1 tbsp	1 tbsp	1 tbsp
Eggs, beaten	3	3	3
Cream	100 ml	4 fl oz	½ cup

1 Roll out the puff pastry to 4 mm/⅙ inch thick. Dust it with the grated cheese and paprika, then flour and roll again to press the ingredients well into the pastry. Prick the pastry with a fork all over to prevent it from rising as a flaky texture is required for this tart. Line a well oiled 23 cm/9 inch baking tin with the pastry, trim the edges. (The leftovers can be used for other dishes.)

2 In a wok or frying pan, heat the oil and stir fry the onion and garlic for 1 minute. Add the tomato pulp, olives and French beans. Cook for 1 minute. Season to taste and add the basil. Cool the mixture in a bowl.

3 In a smaller bowl, blend the eggs and cream and add to the vegetables.

4 Fill the pastry case with the egg vegetable mixture. Bake in the preheated oven at 220C°/450F°/gas mark 7 for 25 minutes. Serve hot or cold with green salad.

Fried Coconut Cream Delight

Serves 6
Preparation 15 minutes, plus chilling
Cooking time 3-5 minutes

This delicate rum flavoured speciality, which I created while working in a luxury hotel in Jamaica, has been a firm favourite for fun-loving party goers.

	Metric	Imperial	American
Fresh coconut milk or water and desiccated coconut (see method)	450 ml	¾ pint	2 cups
Butter	5 tbsp	5 tbsp	5 tbsp
Plain (all-purpose) flour	225 g	8 oz	2 cups
Salt and black pepper	¼ tsp	¼ tsp	¼ tsp
Sugar	1 tsp	1 tsp	1 tsp
Eggs	4	4	4
Egg yolks	4	4	4
Desiccated (shredded) coconut and breadcrumbs	225 g	8 oz	8 oz
White rum	50 ml	2 fl oz	¼ cup
Oil for deep frying			

1 Either use the fresh coconut milk or boil 600 ml/ 1 pint/2½ cups water with 75 g/3 oz/1 cup of desiccated coconut. Liquidize, then strain.

2 Heat 2 tbsp of the butter in a saucepan, add 2 tbsp of the flour to form a roux and cook for 30 seconds only. Gradually stir in the coconut milk and simmer until thick. Season with salt, pepper and sugar.

3 Beat 3 whole eggs and 2 egg yolks in a bowl. Add to the white sauce. Bring to the boil for 2 minutes to thicken more. Remove from the heat. Add the rum.

4 Well coat a tray with butter and oil, pour in the custard mixture. Cool completely, then chill for 30 minutes. Turn onto a clean pastry board and cut into neat squares.

5 Sprinkle the desiccated coconut mixed with crumbs onto a tray. Place the remaining eggs in another shallow dish and put the flour on another plate. First dip each set custard in seasoned flour, then in beaten egg, and finally coat in coconut crumbs.

6 Heat the oil to 190°C/375°F and deep fry the custard fritters for 30 seconds only until golden. Drain well and serve on plates with lettuce leaves.

Poached Egg Florentine

Serves 4
Preparation 10 minutes
Cooking time 8 minutes

Eggs can be poached in salted water in a deep metal tray, adding 2 tablespoons of distilled white vinegar to the water for rapid coagulation. After poaching, the eggs are trimmed and rinsed in plain hot salted water. This is the method used by chefs. However, I think the egg poacher method is easier and keeps the eggs in good shape.

	Metric	Imperial	American
White sauce (see page 27)	300 ml	½ pint	1¼ cups
Egg yolk	1	1	1
Gruyère cheese, grated	50 g	2 oz	½ cup
Salt and pepper			
Cooked leaf spinach	225 g	8 oz	8 oz
Butter	4 tbsp	4 tbsp	4 tbsp
Eggs	4	4	4
Grated Parmesan cheese	2 tbsp	2 tbsp	2 tbsp
Paprika	1 tsp	1 tsp	1 tsp

1 Prepare the mornay sauce. Reheat the white sauce with the egg yolk and grated cheese. Season to taste. Keep hot in a double saucepan.

2 Heat the spinach with a little butter and season to taste. Fill four small earthenware dishes with spinach. Keep hot.

3 Melt 1 tablespoon of butter in each egg poaching cup. Drop a fresh egg into each one. Cover and poach for about 6 minutes until the egg white is firm but egg yolks remain soft.

4 Slip each egg on top of the spinach. Coat with a little cheese sauce. Sprinkle over grated cheese and paprika. Glaze under the grill (broiler) to brown the cheese for 30 seconds.

Broad Beans and Carrot Custard Pie

Serves 6
Preparation 15 minutes
Cooking time 45 minutes

Broad beans tend to be tough and for this reason I suggest the removal of the skin of the bean after it has been parboiled for 5 minutes. It will also improve the appearance.

	Metric	Imperial	American
Broad (lima or fava) beans, podded	225 g	8 oz	8 oz
Baby carrots, washed and diced	225 g	8 oz	8 oz
Piece of fresh ginger, peeled and chopped	1	1	1
Honey	3 tbsp	3 tbsp	3 tbsp
Parsley, chopped	3 tbsp	3 tbsp	3 tbsp
Single (light) cream	600 ml	1 pint	2½ cups
Eggs, beaten	3	3	3
Salt and pepper			
Ground aniseed	1 tsp	1 tsp	1 tsp

1 Boil the broad beans for 5 minutes. Refresh in cold water, drain and remove the outer skin from each bean.

2 Blanch the carrots for 5 minutes in salted water. Drain.

3 Liquidize the ginger with the honey and 5 tablespoons of hot water.

4 In a bowl, combine the cream, beaten eggs and honey mixture. Season to taste, adding the aniseed powder.

5 Butter a 1 litre/2 pint shallow baking dish and half fill it with carrots and skinned broad beans. Top up with the egg and cream mixture.

6 Place in a deep tray half filled with hot water. Bake in the oven at 200°C/400°F/gas mark 6 for 45 minutes. Alternatively, use individual pie dishes 150 ml/¼ pint/ ⅔ cup capacity each.

Leek and Almond Cream

Serves 4
Preparation 10 minutes, plus standing
Cooking time 20 minutes

	Metric	Imperial	American
Medium leeks, white parts only, sliced	450 g	1 lb	1 lb
Butter	3 tbsp	3 tbsp	3 tbsp
Skinned almonds	150 g	6 oz	1 cup
Single (light) cream	150 ml	5 fl oz	⅔ cup
Eggs, beaten	4	4	4
Salt	¼ tsp	¼ tsp	¼ tsp
Pepper	¼ tsp	¼ tsp	¼ tsp
Grated nutmeg	¼ tsp	¼ tsp	¼ tsp
Gruyère or Emmenthal cheese	50 g	2 oz	½ cup
Slice of bread, cubed	1	1	1

1 Wash the sliced leeks and drain. Heat the butter in a shallow pan and stir fry the leeks for 2 minutes, without colouring. Add the almonds and cook for 1 minute more. Remove from the heat.

2 In a bowl, blend the cream and beaten eggs and soak the bread cubes in this mixture. Season to taste. Add the cooked leeks and almonds. Leave to absorb the flavours for 20 minutes.

3 Fill four individual 150 ml/¼ pint/⅔ cup well buttered ramekin dishes with the leek mixture. Sprinkle with grated cheese. Bake in a shallow tray, half filled with water, in the oven at 190°C/375°F/gas mark 5 for 20 minutes.

— CHAPTER EIGHT —

Pulses

* *

Pulses are also called legumes; these include beans, lentils, peas, mung beans, alfalfa, aduki or red soya bean, plus sprouts or germinated shoots.

They are rich in protein and the B vitamins, thiamin and nicotic acid. String beans, runner beans and sugar peas are eaten in the pod and have a similar composition to other green vegetables. A portion of baked beans contains as much protein as an egg. All pulses need the reinforcement of cheese and egg to provide the full quota of essential amino acids.

On the cooking procedure; most split beans, peas and lentils need very little soaking, but soya and other beans have to be soaked in water. Distilled water should be used in areas where the tap water is hard. When soaked and cooked in hard water, the beans tend to crack open, even if bicarbonate of soda is added to the water.

The fresher the beans the better, but dry beans need to be soaked overnight and they take two hours to cook at simmering point. Hence the convenience of buying tinned baked beans.

Lentil Platter aux Petits Legumes

Serves 4
Preparation 10 minutes, plus soaking
Cooking time 20 minutes

	Metric	Imperial	American
Green lentils	150 g	5 oz	⅔ cup
Butter	3 tbsp	3 tbsp	3 tbsp
Cloves of garlic, chopped	2	2	2
Salt and pepper			
Olive oil	2 tbsp	2 tbsp	2 tbsp
Wine vinegar	1 tbsp	1 tbsp	1 tbsp
Pickling onions, peeled	8	8	8
Baby carrots, scraped	16	16	16
Baby sweetcorns	4	4	4
Honey	2 tbsp	2 tbsp	2 tbsp
Mangetout, topped and tailed	16	16	16

1 Soak the green lentils for 25 minutes – this will help in keeping their shape. Simmer gently for 16 minutes. Drain. Add 1 tbsp butter and 1 clove of chopped garlic. Season to taste. Add 1 tbsp oil and vinegar.

2 In a wok, heat 2 tbsp of butter and the remaining 1 tbsp oil and stir fry the pickled onions, carrots and sweetcorn for 2 minutes. Add 8 tbsp water and boil for 5 minutes until liquid is evaporated.

3 Add the honey and mangetout and cook for 2 more minutes. Season to taste. On four plates spoon the hot green lentils and surround with vegetables, arranged decoratively.

Galette de Petits Pois à la Française

Serves 4
Preparation 15 minutes
Cooking time 20 minutes

	Metric	Imperial	American
Unbaked pastry flan case (shell)	20 cm	8 inch	8 inch

Filling

	Metric	Imperial	American
Fresh or frozen petits pois	125 g	5 oz	¾ cup
Spring onions (scallions)	8	8	8
Honey	2 tbsp	2 tbsp	2 tbsp
Salt and black pepper			
Butter	1 tbsp	1 tbsp	1 tbsp
Flour	1 tbsp	1 tbsp	1 tbsp
Double (heavy) cream	100 ml	4 fl oz	½ cup
Eggs, beaten	2	2	2
Shredded lettuce leaves	75 g	3 oz	3 oz
Chopped fresh tarragon	½ tsp	½ tsp	½ tsp
Chopped fresh mint	1 tbsp	1 tbsp	1 tbsp

1 Boil the peas and spring onions in 300 ml/½ pint/ 1¼ cups of salted water for 5 minutes. Stir in the honey. Season to taste.

2 Cream the butter and flour to a paste. Melt this paste into the hot pea liquid mixture. Boil for 4 more minutes, then remove from heat and allow to cool.

3 Blend the cream and beaten eggs and add to the cold pea mixture with the shredded lettuce, chopped tarragon and mint. Season to taste.

4 Fill the flan case with the mixture. Bake in the oven at 200°C/400°F/gas mark 6 for 20 minutes. When set, serve hot or cold with lettuce salad.

Mexican Bean Fiesta

Serves 4
Preparation 15 minutes
Cooking time 2 hours

	Metric	Imperial	American
Michigan navy or haricot beans	125 g	5 oz	1 cup
Distilled water	1.2 ltrs	2 pints	5 cups
Corn oil	4 tbsp	4 tbsp	4 tbsp
Medium red onion, chopped	1	1	1
Red pepper, seeded and diced	1	1	1
Stalk of celery, diced	1	1	1
Stalk of fennel, diced	1	1	1
Sweetcorn kernels, frozen or canned	75 g	3 oz	⅔ cup
Cloves of garlic, chopped	2	2	2
Tomatoes, skinned, seeded and chopped	4	4	4
Basil leaves, chopped	6	6	6
Green chilli, chopped	1	1	1
Cornflour (cornstarch)	1 tbsp	1 tbsp	1 tbsp
Water	8 tbsp	8 tbsp	8 tbsp
Yeast extract	1 tbsp	1 tbsp	1 tbsp
Salt and pepper			
Honey	1 tbsp	1 tbsp	1 tbsp
Grated cheddar cheese	4 tbsp	4 tbsp	4 tbsp

1 Soak the beans in distilled water for 6 hours. Wash in plenty of fresh water. Place the beans in a metal casserole fitted with a lid and cover with the distilled water. Bring to the boil. Remove any scum, cover and bake in the oven at 180°C/350°F/gas mark 4 for 2 hours.

2 In a wok, heat the oil and stir fry the onion, pepper, celery, fennel and sweetcorn kernels for 4 minutes. Add the garlic and cook for 30 seconds, then blend in the tomatoes, basil leaves and chilli. Simmer for five minutes.

3 In a cup mix the cornflour and cold water, add to the boiling ingredients. Cook for 4 minutes. Dilute the yeast extract and season to taste. Add the honey.

4 Drain the beans and mix them into the sauce. Serve in individual soup terrines. Sprinkle with grated cheese and brown under the grill (broiler).

Chickpea and Spinach Casserole

Serves 4
Preparation 5 minutes
Cooking time 5-8 minutes

As dry chickpeas require soaking overnight and need 2 hours to cook, it is simpler to use canned chickpeas.

	Metric	Imperial	American
Fresh spinach, stems removed, washed and drained	450 g	1 lb	1 lb
Melted butter and oil	2 tbsp	2 tbsp	2 tbsp
Clove of garlic, chopped	1	1	1
Can chickpeas (garbanzos)	225 g	8 oz	8 oz
Feta cheese, cut into cubes	100 g	4 oz	1 cup
Salt and freshly milled black pepper			
Sour cream	100 ml	4 fl oz	½ cup

1 Shred the spinach leaves. Heat the butter and oil in a saucepan and cook the spinach for 4 minutes.

2 Add the chickpeas and feta cheese. Season to taste and stir in the sour cream just before serving. This casserole could be served with plain boiled noodles with plenty of grated cheese.

Butter Bean and Rice Cakes

Serves 4
Preparation 10 minutes
Cooking time 5 minutes

Fresh butter or lima beans, boiled and flavoured with butter, are as delicious as the best flageolet beans. Processed in tins, they are sold as butter beans. In this dish, the butter beans have been pounded to a paste with cooked rice, then shallow fried in butter. Ideal for party snacks.

	Metric	Imperial	American
Can butter (lima) beans, drained	125 g	5 oz	5 oz
Cold pilaf with saffron (see page 116)	125 g	5 oz	5 oz
Eggs, beaten	2	2	2
Salt and black pepper			
Seasoned flour			
Oil for shallow frying	6 tbsp	6 tbsp	6 tbsp

1 Mince or pound the beans and cooked rice to a paste. Blend the paste with the beaten eggs. Season and divide the mixture into four balls. Flatten into cakes and coat in seasoned flour.

2 Heat the oil in a shallow pan and fry the cakes for 1 minute on each side until golden. Serve on a plate with watercress and chicory leaves.

Terrine de Légumes aux Champignons Blancs

Serves 6
Preparation 15 minutes, plus setting
Cooking time 10 minutes

	Metric	Imperial	American
Carrot, diced in 4 mm/⅙ inch cubes	50 g	2 oz	½ cup
Turnip, diced in 4 mm/⅙ inch cubes	50 g	2 oz	½ cup
French beans, diced in 4 mm/⅙ inch cubes	50 g	2 oz	½ cup
Fresh peas	50 g	2 oz	½ cup
Sweetcorn kernels	50 g	2 oz	½ cup
Button mushrooms, sliced	100 g	4 oz	1 cup
Butter	3 tbsp	3 tbsp	3 tbsp
Honey	2 tbsp	2 tbsp	2 tbsp
Celery seeds	1 tsp	1 tsp	1 tsp
Dried thyme	pinch	pinch	pinch
Binding cream mixture			
Butter	1 tbsp	1 tbsp	1 tbsp
Flour	1 tbsp	1 tbsp	1 tbsp
Milk	300 ml	½ pint	1¼ cups
Medium onion, chopped	1	1	1
Cream cheese	150 g	5 oz	¾ cup
Powdered gelatine (unflavoured gelatine)	15 g	½ oz	½ oz
Salt	1 tsp	1 tsp	1 tsp
White pepper	¼ tsp	¼ tsp	¼ tsp
Grated nutmeg	¼ tsp	¼ tsp	¼ tsp

1 Blanch the macedoine of vegetables in boiling salted water for 3 minutes only. Drain and refresh in cold water. Drain again.

2 In a wok, heat the butter and honey and stir fry the vegetables and mushrooms for 2 minutes only. Add the celery seeds and thyme. Remove from the heat.

3 For the cream sauce, heat the butter and flour for 1 minute, to form a white roux. Stir in the milk and chopped onion. Simmer for 5 minutes until the sauce is thick.

4 Dissolve the gelatine and blend in the cream cheese. Season with salt, white pepper and grated nutmeg. In a bowl, combine the cream mixture with the cooked vegetables.

5 Spoon mixture into six individual ramekin dishes. Allow to set in the refrigerator for 2 hours. Turn onto lettuce leaves.

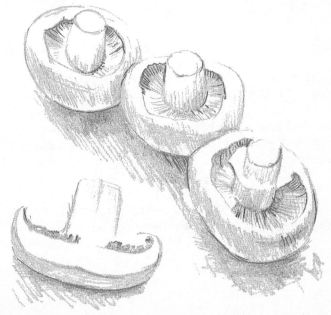

Deep Fried Dwarf Beans Milanese

Serves 4
Preparation 5 minutes
Cooking time 15 minutes

Young Dwarf beans are usually boiled in salted water, tossed in butter and served. But there are other tasty ways of serving these beans and the following recipe is ideal served with drinks at a party.

	Metric	Imperial	American
Dwarf beans (French type), trimmed	450 g	1 lb	1 lb
Seasoned flour with 1 tsp salt	100 g	4 oz	1 cup
Eggs, beaten with 2 tbsp water	2	2	2
Oil for frying			
Celery salt or salt			
Chilli pepper			

1 Boil the beans in salted water for 7 minutes. Drain, refresh in cold water. Drain again and pat dry.

2 Tie up the beans in four small bundles with string. Dip the bunches in seasoned flour, then in beaten egg, then again in seasoned flour. Heat the oil to 190°C/375°F and deep fry for 3 minutes. Drain well on absorbent paper.

3 Sprinkle the beans with celery salt and chilli pepper. Remove the strings. Serve with mayonnaise or a tomato dip.

Bean and Potato Boxties

Serves 4
Preparation 5-8 minutes
Cooking time 5 minutes

This is my recommended snack for childrens' parties as most kids seem to like savoury foods as well as sweet foods.

	Metric	Imperial	American
Large potato, peeled	225 g	8 oz	8 oz
French beans, boiled and cut into strips	150 g	5 oz	1¼ cups
Beaten eggs	2	2	2
Flour	2 tbsp	2 tbsp	2 tbsp
Oil for shallow frying			
Salt			

1 Grate the potato coarsely, place in a cloth and press out the liquid.

2 In a bowl, mix the grated potato with the cooked beans, beaten egg and flour.

3 Heat the oil in a shallow pan and add spoonfuls of the mixture, frying four at a time. Fry on both sides for 2½ minutes.

4 Drain on absorbent paper and season with salt. Serve hot with tomato dip, ketchup or any other bottled sauces.

Lentil Cakes with Chicory

Serves 4
Preparation 10 minutes
Cooking time 30 minutes

There is no need to soak green lentils as they cook quickly. From Biblical times this legume has been a source of protein, good enough to sustain life. It can be made into tasty soups, loaves and as a cake it is well worth a try.

	Metric	Imperial	American
Green lentils	225 g	8 oz	1 cup
Carrot, diced	1	1	1
Onion, chopped	25 g	1 oz	¼ cup
Long grain rice	50 g	2 oz	⅓ cup
Eggs, beaten	2	2	2
Cloves of garlic, chopped	2	2	2
Wholemeal flour	25 g	1 oz	¼ cup
Salt and black pepper			
Seasoned flour	3 tbsp	3 tbsp	3 tbsp
Oil for shallow frying			
Chicory chicons (Belgian endives)	4	4	4

Dressing

	Metric	Imperial	American
Olive oil	3 tbsp	3 tbsp	3 tbsp
Wine vinegar	1 tbsp	1 tbsp	1 tbsp
Made mustard	¾ tsp	¾ tsp	¾ tsp
Salt and pepper			
Chopped fresh parsley	2 tbsp	2 tbsp	2 tbsp

1 Boil the lentils, carrot and onion in salted water for 25 minutes. Drain and mince to a purée.

2 Meanwhile, boil the rice for 20 minutes. Drain and blend into the lentil purée. Add the eggs, garlic and flour. Season to taste.

3 Shape the mixture like scones. Coat in seasoned flour.

4 Heat the oil in a shallow pan and fry for 3 minutes on each side until golden.

5 Cut the chicory in thin slices. Wash and drain. Blend the salad dressing ingredients and sprinkle over the salad. Serve one lentil cake per portion with this salad, sprinked with parsley.

Indian Chickpeas and Fried Cheese Dumplings

Serves 8
Preparation 15 minutes
Cooking time about 1¼ hours

Caraway seeds and lime add a pleasant taste to chick peas in this delicious protein-rich Indian vegetable dish.

	Metric	Imperial	American
Chickpeas (garbanzo beans)	450 g	1 lb	1 lb
Water	1.7 ltrs	3 pints	7½ cups
Tea bag Ceylon tea	1	1	1
Each ground cinnamon, nutmeg and black pepper	½ tsp	½ tsp	½ tsp
Caraway seeds	2 tsp	2 tsp	2 tsp
Juice and grated rind of lemon	1	1	1
Juice and grated rind of lime	1	1	1
Salt	1 tsp	1 tsp	1 tsp
Ginger in syrup, cut into strips	25 g	1 oz	2 tbsp
Fresh coriander leaves, chopped	150 g	6 oz	6 oz
Sunflower oil or butter	7 tbsp	7 tbsp	7 tbsp
Tomatoes, skinned, seeded and cut into wedges	2	2	2
Cream cheese	225 g	8 oz	1 cup
Seasoned flour	4 tbsp	4 tbsp	4 tbsp
Egg, beaten	1	1	1
Breadcrumbs	8 tbsp	8 tbsp	8 tbsp
Oil for deep frying			

1 Boil the chick peas in the water for 5 minutes, brew a tea bag in the liquid for 5 minutes, then remove. Continue simmering the chick peas for another hour or so until tender. Drain the chick peas.

2 Blend all the spices and seeds, lemon and lime juice. Season to taste and add the ginger strips and most of the coriander leaves.

3 Heat the oil or butter and toss the mixture to develop a good spice flavour. Add the tomato and cook for 1 minute more.

4 Shape the cream cheese into balls as big as walnuts. Coat in seasoned flour, beaten eggs, then crumbs. Deep fry in oil until golden for 2 minutes.

5 Serve three cheese balls per person with a scoop of the chick pea mixture. Sprinkle over remaining chopped coriander leaves.

Courge aux Flageolets

Serves 4
Preparation 10 minutes
Cooking time 2 hours,
*   30 minutes if using canned beans*

One of the most tasty haricot beans is without question the flageolet variety. The beans are greenish when fresh. In combination with thin French beans blended with a good lemon dressing, it makes a superb starter.

	Metric	Imperial	American
Medium marrow (squash)	900 g	2 lb	2 lb
Filling			
Flageolet beans, dried (or canned)	225 g	8 oz	8 oz
Dwarf French beans, trimmed and cut in small pieces	225 g	8 oz	8 oz
Dressing			
Juice of lemon	1	1	1
Small onion, chopped	1	1	1
Made mustard	1 tsp	1 tsp	1 tsp
Olive oil	3 tbsp	3 tbsp	3 tbsp
White pickling vinegar	1 tsp	1 tsp	1 tsp
Salt and pepper			
Chopped fresh parsley	3 tbsp	3 tbsp	3 tbsp
Bunch of chives, snipped	1	1	1

1 Peel the marrow and divide into two lengthwise, then in two again across. Remove the seeds to hollow the cavities. Boil the pieces in salted water for 8-10 minutes, then drain and pat dry on a cloth. To keep the pieces in shape, do not overcook.

2 Boil the flageolet beans for 1½ hours if dried, using distilled water preferably. If using canned, reheat and cook for 10 minutes and drain.

3 Boil the green beans for 8 minutes. Refresh and drain.

4 Combine the two beans in a bowl. Blend the dressing ingredients and toss the beans in it.

5 To serve, fill each marrow cavity with the beans. Place on plates and sprinkle over chopped parsley and fresh snipped chives.

Bean Sprouts and Fennel with Egg Noodles

Serves 4
Preparation 10 minutes
Cooking time 12-14 minutes

	Metric	Imperial	American
Thin egg noodles	225 g	8 oz	8 oz
Bulb fennel, cut in thin julienne shreds	1	1	1
Oil and butter	3 tbsp	3 tbsp	3 tbsp
Spring onions (scallions) with green stems, sliced slantwise	6	6	6
Cloves of garlic, chopped	2	2	2
Small piece of fresh root ginger, chopped	1	1	1
Ring of pineapple, cut into thin strips	1	1	1
Cooked red beans (canned)	100 g	4 oz	⅔ cup
Bean sprouts	225 g	8 oz	4 cups
Soya sauce	1 tbsp	1 tbsp	1 tbsp
Distilled vinegar	1 tbsp	1 tbsp	1 tbsp
Honey	1 tbsp	1 tbsp	1 tbsp
Salt and pepper			

1 Boil the noodles for 5 minutes and drain.

2 Blanch the fennel strips for 2 minutes and drain.

3 In a wok or frying pan, heat the oil and butter and stir fry the spring onions for 2 minutes. Add the garlic and ginger and toss for 30 seconds, then add fennel, noodles, pineapple and red beans. Lastly add the bean sprouts. Toss.

4 Add the soya sauce, vinegar, honey and salt and pepper. Reheat for 3 minutes only. Serve with fried rice on large plates.

Pain de Haricot, Lentille et Pois Vert

Serves 6
Preparation 8 minutes
Cooking time 30 minutes

	Metric	Imperial	American
Cooked haricot (navy) beans	150 g	5 oz	⅔ cup
Cooked green lentils	150 g	5 oz	⅔ cup
Cooked split green peas	150 g	5 oz	⅔ cup
Blue cheese, mashed	50 g	2 oz	½ cup
Butter	50 g	2 oz	¼ cup
Celery seeds	1 tbsp	1 tbsp	1 tbsp
Chopped peanuts	50 g	2 oz	½ cup
Eggs, beaten	4	4	4
Salt and black pepper			
Shredded green cabbage, boiled	225 g	8 oz	8 oz

1 Mince all the pulses to a purée. Combine the paste in a bowl with the blue cheese, celery seeds, butter, chopped nuts and beaten eggs. Season to taste with about 1 level tsp salt and ½ tsp black pepper.

2 Oil an oblong baking tin, capacity 750 ml/1¼ pints/ 3 cups. Fill with mixture to the top and cover with greased paper. Bake in the oven at 200°C/400°F/gas mark 6 for 30 minutes.

3 Cool and turn onto a board. Cut in thick slices and serve with shredded green boiled cabbage. Serve with mayonnaise or French dressing.

Sweet and Sour Runner Beans

Serves 4
Preparation 10 minutes
Cooking time 15 minutes

	Metric	Imperial	American
Young runner beans	450 g	1 lb	1 lb
Oil			
Honey	3 tbsp	3 tbsp	3 tbsp
Distilled vinegar	2 tbsp	2 tbsp	2 tbsp
Tomato purée	1 tbsp	1 tbsp	1 tbsp
Salt and black pepper			
Pinch of Chinese spices			
Toasted peanuts	100 g	4 oz	1 cup
Slices of Cheddar Cheese	4	4	4

1 With a potato peeler, shave each side of the beans to remove the stringy edges. Cut off the tops and tails. Cut the beans into diagonal lengths no shorter than 4 cm/ 1½ inches. Boil in salted water for 8 minutes.

2 In a wok or frying pan, heat the oil and honey. Stir fry the beans for 2 minutes. Add the vinegar and tomato purée and boil for 3 more minutes.

3 Season with salt and pepper and a pinch of Chinese spices (anis seeds, cinnamon, clove and grated nutmeg). Add the toasted peanuts and serve with a slice of cheese.

— CHAPTER NINE —

Potato Dishes

* * * * * * * * * * * * * * * * * * *

Potatoes are extremely versatile and there are numerous dishes — from starters to main courses to savoury pies — for which they form the base.

The main thing to remember when using potatoes is always to keep them in cold water until you are ready to cook them, if you do not they will blacken and look very unattractive. Remember, too, that waxy potatoes are best for frying and mealy potatoes are best for mashing.

Potatoes can be used in so many ways and a number of suggestions can be found in the following chapter, but do not forget that new potatoes simply peeled, boiled and served hot with yoghurt or a lemon dressing is probably the most delicious potato dish of all.

Clapshot of Potato and Swede

Serves 4
Preparation 10 minutes
Cooking time 11-15 minutes

This is one of the most popular potato pies in Scotland. A meal in itself, or it can be served with hard Scottish cheese or curd cheese.

	Metric	Imperial	American
Mealy potatoes, peeled and sliced	450 g	1 lb	1 lb
Swede (ruta baga) or turnip, peeled and cut into small cubes	450 g	1 lb	1 lb
Medium onion, chopped	1	1	1
Butter	50 g	2 oz	¼ cup
Salt and white pepper			
Chives, snipped			

1 Boil the potato, swede and onion for about 12-15 minutes, removing any scum as it rises.

2 Drain and mash to a fine purée, then pass thorugh a sieve. Flavour with butter, salt and pepper. Present in individual pie dishes sprinkled with snipped chives.

Pomme Farçie au Fromage Blanc

Serves 4
Preparation 10 minutes
Cooking time 1 hour

	Metric	Imperial	American
Large potatoes, 225 g/8 oz each	2	2	2
Butter	2 tbsp	2 tbsp	2 tbsp
Filling			
Cream cheese	100 g	4 oz	1 cup
Yoghurt	4 tbsp	4 tbsp	4 tbsp
Salt and white pepper			
Chives, snipped			

1 Wash and scrub the potatoes and wipe dry. Cut in half lengthwise. With the point of a knife, make criss cross indentations over the pulp. (This will speed the baking). Brush the top with the butter and wrap in foil.

2 Bake at 200°C/400°F/gas mark 6 for 45 minutes to 1 hour. When baked, remove the foil and scoop out the hot pulp. Pass it through a sieve if possible, otherwise mash it well.

3 In a bowl, blend the hot mashed potato with the cream cheese, yoghurt and seasoning. Spoon the mixture back into the potato skins. Smooth it into a domed shape with a palette knife. Reheat for 5 minutes, then sprinkle the top with chives and serve.

Casserole de Pommes en Ragôut Oriental

Serves 6
Preparation 10 minutes
Cooking time 25-35 minutes

	Metric	Imperial	American
Oil and butter	3 tbsp	3 tbsp	3 tbsp
Medium onion, chopped	1	1	1
Cloves of garlic, chopped	2	2	2
Curry powder	2 tbsp	2 tbsp	2 tbsp
Red pepper, split, seeded and cut into 2.5 cm/ 1 inch squares	1	1	1
Green chilli, sliced	1	1	1
Stalk of celery, cut in wedges	1	1	1
French beans, trimmed, cut in small pieces	100 g	4 oz	⅔ cup
Fresh peas	100 g	4 oz	⅔ cup
Carrot, peeled and diced 1 cm/½ inch thick	1	1	1

	Metric	Imperial	American
Turnip, peeled and diced	1	1	1
Sweetcorn kernels	100 g	4 oz	1 cup
New small potatoes, scraped	450 g	1 lb	1 lb
Very small onions,	12	12	12
15 g/½ oz each			
Sprigs of cauliflower	6	6	6
Salt			
Tomato purée	2 tbsp	2 tbsp	2 tbsp
Cooked haricot beans	100 g	4 oz	⅔ cup
Fresh chopped parsley	3 tbsp	3 tbsp	3 tbsp

1 In a heavy based pan, capacity 3 litres/6 pints/7 pints, heat the oil and butter and stir fry the onion and garlic for 30 seconds. Add the curry powder, red pepper, chilli and all the other vegetables.

2 Cover with water, about 1 litre/1¾ pints/3¾ cups and boil gently for 20-30 minutes. Season with salt, then add the tomato purée and cooked beans. Reheat for 5 minutes. Serve in soup plates with some of the liquid. Sprinkle with chopped parsley.

Gratin des Deux Pommes aux Amandes

Serves 4
Preparation 10 minutes
Cooking time 30 minutes

Here is another combination of potatoes and apples which have pleased many country gourmets. Use dessert apples for this kind of dish as they have better texture than cooking apples.

	Metric	Imperial	American
Waxy potatoes, small	450 g	1 lb	1 lb
Dessert apples, Cox's Orange Pippin	4	4	4
Butter	100 g	4 oz	½ cup
Shallots, chopped	2	2	2
Salt and white pepper			
Grated nutmeg			
Honey, heated	4 tbsp	4 tbsp	4 tbsp
Flaked almonds, toasted	100 g	4 oz	1 cup
Icing (confectioner's) sugar, to sprinkle			

1 Peel the potatoes and cut into 4 mm/⅙ inch thick rounds. Peel and core the apples and cut into rings.

2 Put 25 g/1 oz/2 tbsp of butter in the bottom of four 250 ml/½ pint/1 cup pie dishes with 1 tsp of chopped shallots. Arrange the apple and potato slices in alternate rows. Season with salt, white pepper and nutmeg. Brush the top of each pie with hot honey. Ladle 6 tbsp of water onto each pie.

3 Bake in the oven at 200°C/400°F/gas mark 6 for 30 minutes. Brush with melted butter and honey from time to time to keep the tops golden. Sprinkle with toasted flaked almonds just before serving and dust the top with icing (confectioner's) sugar. This is not a dessert but a snack for those who like a sweet tasting potato pie. Serve with lettuce.

Courge aux Pommes Savoyarde

Serves 4
Preparation 8 minutes
Cooking time 20 minutes

Some old fashioned potato dishes take too long to cook and very often are not well presented. This is a nouvelle cuisine way of making this dish more attractive without losing character.

	Metric	Imperial	American
Medium size marrow (squash)	1	1	1
Watercress to garnish			
Filling			
Medium size waxy potatoes, peeled	225 g	8 oz	8 oz
Butter for frying			
Cloves of garlic	3	3	3
Cream	150 ml	¼ pint	⅔ cup
Salt and white pepper			
Grated nutmeg			

1 Cut the marrow in two lengthwise and in two again, making four portions. Scoop out the seeds with a spoon. Scrape the outer skin with a potato peeler.

2 Partly cook for 3 minutes only in boiling salted water. Remove, drain and pat dry. Place the marrow pieces on a baking tray.

3 Peel the potatoes and cut in 0.5 cm/¼ inch thick slices. Boil the potato slices for 4 minutes only so that they retain their texture without breaking.

4 In a small saucepan or pan, heat the butter and shallow fry the garlic for 30 seconds only. Pour the content of this into the cavity of each marrow case. Arrange the parboiled potato slices onto each marrow, overlapping each other. Coat the potatoes with cream. Season with salt, pepper and grated nutmeg.

5 Bake in the oven at 200°C/400°F/gas mark 6 for 20 minutes at the most. Serve on four plates as a main course. Garnish with a bunch of watercress.

Goulash of Potato and Onion in Paprika Sauce

Serves 4
Preparation 5 minutes
Cooking time 25 minutes

	Metric	Imperial	American
Butter and oil	4 tbsp	4 tbsp	4 tbsp
Pickling onions, 15 g/½ oz each	225 g	8 oz	8 oz
Red pepper, split, seeded and diced	1	1	1
New potatoes of even size	450 g	1 lb	1 lb
Paprika	1 tbsp	1 tbsp	1 tbsp
Tomato purée	2 tbsp	2 tbsp	2 tbsp
Salt and pepper			
Caraway seeds	1 tsp	1 tsp	1 tsp
Water	600 ml	1 pint	2½ cups
Toasted hazelnuts	75 g	3 oz	¾ cup
Fresh, coarsely chopped coriander	3 tbsp	3 tbsp	3 tbsp
Sour cream	150 ml	¼ pint	⅔ cup

1 In a large heavy based pan, heat the butter and oil and stir fry the onions for 3 minutes until lightly browned. Add the red pepper and cook for 1 minute. Put in the potatoes and paprika and toss well.

2 Cover the vegetables with the water. Add the tomato purée, seasoning and caraway seeds. Boil gently for 18-20 minutes.

3 Remove from the heat and blend the sour cream into the liquid. Sprinkle with toasted hazelnuts and chopped coriander just before serving.

Artichoke, Cucumber and Potato Flash

Serves 4
Preparation 10 minutes
Cooking time 20 minutes

Globe artichokes are plentiful in France, Italy and Spain, and are used for starters or salad. The best part of the artichoke is the bottom fleshy base which holds the leaves together.

	Metric	Imperial	American
Artichoke bottoms, see method	4	4	4
Lemon juice			
Vinegar	1 tsp	1 tsp	1 tsp
Oil and butter for shallow frying	75 g	3 oz	6 tbsp
Peeled potatoes, cut into 1 cm/½ inch cubes	225 g	8 oz	8 oz
Small cucumber, peeled and cut in thick chunks	1	1	1
Cashew nuts, coarsely chopped	75 g	3 oz	¾ cup
Salt and black pepper			
Chopped fresh parsley	3 tbsp	3 tbsp	3 tbsp

1 Although the small part of the leaves are edible in this dish, only the bottom is used. To prepare the artichokes, cut out all the leaves, remove and discard the choke, then cut the bottom all round for an even shape. Cut the bottom in four quarters. Rub with lemon and boil for 10 minutes in salted water with 1 tsp of vinegar. Canned artichoke hearts are available.

2 Heat the oil and butter in a shallow pan and fry the potatoes first as they take the longest to cook through. Cook for 5 minutes over low heat, tossing from time to time. Add the cooked artichoke bottoms and stir.

3 Finally add the cucumber chunks and cook for 1 minute only. Add the cashew nuts. Season with salt and pepper. During the cooking, the sautéeing and stirring process must be continuous to avoid over-browning. Drain and serve on plates.

Potato and Pistachio Venetian Cakes

Serves 4
Preparation 15 minutes
Cooking time about 1¼ hours

These kind of round croquettes are very popular for drinks parties and can be made smaller if required.

	Metric	Imperial	American
Large baking potatoes, 200 g/7 oz each	3	3	3
Egg yolks	2	2	2
Butter	25 g	1 oz	2 tbsp
Salt and pepper			
Pistachio nuts, skinned	75 g	3 oz	¾ cup
Sultanas (seedless white raisins)	75 g	3 oz	½ cup
Coating			
Seasoned flour	6 tbsp	6 tbsp	6 tbsp
Fine cornmeal semolina	75 g	3 oz	½ cup
Powdered Italian macaroons	75 g	3 oz	3 oz
Egg, beaten with 3 tbsp water	1	1	1
Oil for shallow frying	100 ml	4 fl oz	½ cup

1 Wash, scrub and dry the potatoes. Wrap in foil and bake in the oven at 200°C/400°F/gas mark 6 for 1 hour.

2 Prepare three plates, one with seasoned flour, one with cornmeal semolina mixed with powdered macaroons and one with beaten egg and water.

3 When the baked potatoes are cooked, unwrap and cut in half. Scoop out the pulp and sieve it to remove lumps.

4 In a bowl, blend the purée with the egg yolks and butter. Season. Add the pistachio nuts and sultanas. Cool the potato mixture. When cold, divide into 12-16 balls. Roll them in flour and shape them like scones, using a palette knife.

5 Heat oil in a shallow pan. Coat the potato cakes in beaten egg, then in cornmeal mixture. Shallow fry on both sides for 2 minutes until golden brown. Drain and serve with lettuce leaves tossed in lemon dressing.

Button Sprouts, Chestnuts and New Potatoes

Serves 4
Preparation 10 minutes
Cooking time 25 minutes

Boiled Brussels sprouts are not liked by the majority of people who partake of Christmas fare. Yet there are other recipes which do more justice to this much maligned member of the cabbage family. There are fundamental rules to observe to eliminate the bitter taste. Sprouts should be washed with water acidulated with a little vinegar. They should be blanched in salted water for 8 minutes, then refreshed in icy cold water to retain their green colour and lose their bitter taste. Most French cooks will toss the boiled sprouts in butter. It is then traditional to add a few boiled chestnuts during this process and, if by chance, you can get baby new potatoes the size of marbles, then you have a winning threesome.

	Metric	Imperial	American
Button brussels (see method)	225 g	8 oz	8 oz
Distilled vinegar	2 tbsp	2 tbsp	2 tbsp
Baby new potatoes	225 g	8 oz	8 oz
Button onions	225 g	8 oz	8 oz
Butter	100 g	4 oz	½ cup
Small chestnuts, boiled	225 g	8 oz	8 oz
Salt and black pepper			
Grated Parmesan cheese	50 g	2 oz	½ cup

1 Select sprouts that are no bigger than walnuts. Remove any outer wilted leaves. Cut a cross in the stem part. Wash in cold water with the distilled vinegar. Boil in salted water for 8 minutes. Drain and rinse in very cold water. Drain finally when they are cold. Pat dry and keep on a tray ready to be tossed in butter.

2 Meanwhile, scrape the small potatoes and wash. Boil for 15-18 minutes. Drain.

3 Boil the onions for 4 minutes only. Drain.

4 When ready to serve, heat the butter in a large pan and toss the sprouts, onions, potatoes and chestnuts for 4 minutes. Season to taste. Serve on individual plates and sprinkle with Parmesan cheese. While tossing the mixture you can sprinkle with some flavouring seeds, such as mustard, sesame or caraway.

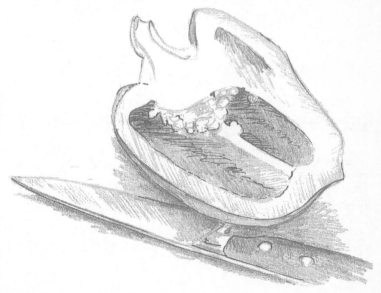

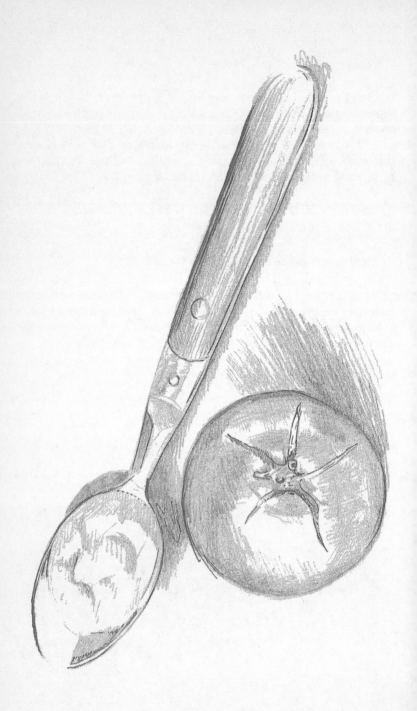

— CHAPTER TEN —

Chinese Celebration Stir Fry Dishes

* * * * * * * * * * * * * * * * * * * *

There is no doubt Chinese food is very popular. These vegetarian dishes have been selected because they use favourite ingredients − pulses, mushrooms and nuts being the most prominent. All of these dishes can be served either with boiled or fried rice or pasta − thin egg noodles, rice vermicelli, butterflies, shells, all kinds of shapes can be used. Soya curd cheese, known as tofu, can be purchased in oriental and health food shops. Each dish has its own sauce including bottled sauces such as soya, tomato ketchup or bought fruit sauce, used in conjunction with stock cubes, vegetable extracts and various fruit juices.

Broccoli and Button Mushroms

Serves 4
Preparation 10 minutes
Cooking time 6 minutes

	Metric	Imperial	American
Broccoli sprigs	225 g	8 oz	8 oz
Button onions, skinned	12	12	12
Bamboo shoots, canned	225 g	8 oz	8 oz
Cashew nuts	150 g	5 oz	1 cup
Sunflower oil	4 tbsp	4 tbsp	4 tbsp
Clove of garlic, chopped	1	1	1
Button mushrooms	225 g	8 oz	2 cups
Tomato juice	100 ml	4 fl oz	½ cup
Soya sauce	1 tbsp	1 tbsp	1 tbsp
Small piece of fresh root ginger, chopped	1	1	1
Water	75 ml	3 fl oz	6 tbsp
Vegetable stock cube	1	1	1
Salt and pepper			
Sugar or honey	½ tsp	½ tsp	½ tsp
Cornflour (cornstarch) blended with 3 tbsp water	1 tsp	1 tsp	1 tsp

1 Prepare the vegetables and have them ready in individual containers. Separate the broccoli into very small sprigs, shorten stalks. Peel the button onions. Cut the bamboo shoots into thin slices, then into strips. Cut the cashew nuts into smaller pieces or leave whole.

2 Heat the oil in a wok or large frying pan. Quickly sauté the vegetables, except the mushrooms, for 3 minutes. Add the garlic, button mushrooms and cashew nuts and stir fry for 30 seconds. Add the tomato juice, soya sauce, ginger, water and stock cube. Boil for 1 minute. Season to taste with salt, pepper and a little sugar.

3 In a cup, blend the cornflour and water, then add to the mixture, stirring, for 1 minute more.

4 Cook for 3 more minutes to bind the whole mixture. Serve hot on four plates.

Jardinierè de Légumes Cantonese Style

Serves 4
Preparation 15 minutes
Cooking time 8 minutes

This recipe is made up of root vegetables, cut into batons the same size.

	Metric	Imperial	American
Carrots	225 g	8 oz	8 oz
Turnips	225 g	8 oz	8 oz
Swedes (rutabagas)	225 g	8 oz	8 oz
Bamboo shoots	150 g	5 oz	5 oz
Celery	225 g	8 oz	8 oz
Large onion	1	1	1
French green beans, trimmed	225 g	8 oz	8 oz
Olive oil	4 tbsp	4 tbsp	4 tbsp
Small piece of fresh root ginger, chopped	1	1	1
Salt and pepper			
Water	100 ml	4 fl oz	½ cup
Vegetable stock cube	1	1	1
Juice and grated rind of lemon	1	1	1
Egg yolks and 2 tbsp water	2	2	2
Cornflour (cornstarch)	1 tsp	1 tsp	1 tsp
Little sugar			
Chinese or cos lettuce leaves			
Sesame seeds, toasted or browned in the oven	2 tbsp	2 tbsp	2 tbsp

1 Cut all the root vegetables into batons, 0.5 cm/¼ inch thick by 5 cm/2 inches long. Blanch the carrots, turnips and swedes for 30 seconds only. Drain well.

2 Cut the large onion in four pieces and divide each one into pieces by separating each layer. Blanch for 30 seconds and drain.

3 Trim the French beans to the same length as the root vegetables. Blanch for 30 seconds. Drain and refresh in iced water. Drain again.

4 In a large wok or pan, heat the oil and ginger, then stir fry all the blanched vegetables for 2 minutes. Season to taste, add the water and stock cube and boil for 3 minutes. Add the bamboo shoots and the juice and grated rind of the lemon. (Use a rinder knife for the lemon.)

5 Drain all the mixture in a colander over a bowl. Collect the juices and place in the pan. Blend the egg yolks and water with the cornflour. Gradually add to the pan and cook for 1 minute, stirring to thicken. At this stage, blend all the ingredients with the sauce. Season to taste with salt, pepper and sugar. Serve on lettuce leaves. Sprinkle the sesame seeds over the vegetables.

Chinese Rainbow of Peppers

Serves 4
Preparation 8 minutes
Cooking time 20 minutes

You can now purchase peppers of different colours — red, yellow, purple, green — which makes this dish very attractive. Chinese spices are made up of anis seed, cinnamon, clove and nutmeg.

	Metric	Imperial	American
Peppers, yellow, red and green, 225 g/8 oz each	3	3	3
Short cut macaroni	225 g	8 oz	8 oz
Olive or walnut oil	4 tbsp	4 tbsp	4 tbsp
Medium onion, cut into strips, 0.5 cm/¼ inch thick	1	1	1
Cloves of garlic, chopped	2	2	2
Mangetout (snow peas)	225 g	8 oz	8 oz
Water	100 ml	4 fl oz	½ cup
Stock cube	1	1	1
Cornflour (cornstarch), blended with 3 tbsp water	1 tsp	1 tsp	1 tsp
Salt and pepper			
Sugar	1 tsp	1 tsp	1 tsp
Chinese spice powder	½ tsp	½ tsp	½ tsp
Grated Cheddar cheese (optional)	100 g	4 oz	1 cup

1 Halve the peppers, remove seeds and membranes. Cut into 5 cm/2 inch lengths, 0.5 cm/¼ inch thick.

2 Boil the macaroni for 12 minutes. Refresh in cold water and drain.

3 Heat the oil in a wok or pan and stir fry the onion, garlic, mangetout and peppers for 2-3 minutes. Add the water and stock cube. Boil for 3 minutes. Thicken with the blended cornflour. Boil for 1 more minute. Season with salt, pepper, sugar and Chinese spices. Serve in individual Chinese bowls. If using, serve grated Cheddar cheese separately.

Tofu Medley of Aubergine, Potato and Celeriac

Serves 4
Preparation 15 minutes, plus marinating
Cooking time 8 minutes

Tofu or soya cheese will absorb any flavour like a sponge, so in a marinade sauce the tofu will be very tasty.

	Metric	Imperial	American
Tofu, cut in 2.5 cm/1 inch cubes	225 g	8 oz	8 oz
Celeriac root, peeled and washed	1	1	1
Large potato, peeled	1	1	1
Aubergine (eggplant), cut in slices	1	1	1
Salt			
Seasoned flour	3 tbsp	3 tbsp	3 tbsp
Eggs, beaten	2	2	2
Sesame seeds	4 tbsp	4 tbsp	4 tbsp
Oil for shallow frying			
Large onion, quartered and separated into layers	1	1	1
Cornflour (cornstarch), blended with 3 tbsp water	1 tsp	1 tsp	1 tsp
Tomato salad with French dressing to serve			

	Metric	Imperial	American
Marinade			
Clove of garlic, chopped	1	1	1
Piece of fresh root ginger, chopped	1	1	1
Pineapple syrup (from can of pineapple)			
Medium sherry	4 tbsp	4 tbsp	4 tbsp
Green chilli, chopped	1	1	1
Salt	½ tsp	½ tsp	½ tsp
Yeast extract	1 tsp	1 tsp	1 tsp

1 Assemble all the ingredients for the marinade in a shallow dish. Add the tofu cubes — leave to marinate for about 1 hour. Drain and keep the liquid for the sauce-making.

2 Cut the celeriac and potato into 2.5 cm×2.5 cm/ 1 inch×1 inch sticks, then cut into thin square slices. Sprinkle salt over the sliced aubergines and leave for 20 minutes. Rinse off the salt and pat dry. Dip the aubergine slices in flour, beaten egg, then coat in sesame seeds.

3 Heat 8 tbsp oil to smoking point and fry the aubergine slices for 1 minute. Drain on absorbent paper.

4 Blanch the celeriac, onion and potato in boiling salted water for 1 minute. Drain and pat dry.

5 Heat oil and fry the tofu for 1 minute until brown, then add the blanched vegetables and marinade sauce. Boil for 1 minute. Thicken with the blended cornflour. Boil for 1 more minute. Season to taste.

6 Serve the tofu mixture on four plates. Garnish with fried aubergines which should be very crisp. Accompany with the salad.

Asparagus, Bean Shoots and Red Bean Assortment

Serves 4
Preparation 10 minutes
Cooking time 15 minutes

	Metric	Imperial	American
Asparagus	225 g	8 oz	8 oz
Spring onions (scallions)	225 g	8 oz	8 oz
Punnet bean sprouts	1	1	1
Macaroni	150 g	5 oz	5 oz
Olive oil	4 tbsp	4 tbsp	4 tbsp
Green chilli, seeded and cut in strips	1	1	1
Medium dry white wine	5 tbsp	5 tbsp	5 tbsp
Chopped fresh root ginger	1 tsp	1 tsp	1 tsp
Caraway or celery seeds	1 tbsp	1 tbsp	1 tbsp
Cooked red beans	225 g	8 oz	8 oz
Salt and pepper			
Mixed green lettuce and salad leaves			
Grapefruits, segmented	2	2	2
Wine vinegar	2 tbsp	2 tbsp	2 tbsp

1 Scrape and trim the asparagus. Cut in small pieces, 3 cm/1¼ inches long. Parboil for 2 minutes in salted water and drain.

2 Trim the onions and cut in 3 cm/1¼ inch long strips with green stems.

3 Wash, rinse and pat dry the bean sprouts.

4 Boil the macaroni for 12 minutes. Rinse and pat dry.

5 Heat the oil in a wok and quickly sauté the onion, chilli and asparagus for 2 minutes. Add the wine, ginger, caraway or celery seeds and macaroni. Toss for 1 more minute, then add the red beans, bean sprouts and seasoning and cook for 1 more minute.

6 Serve in four bowls lined with salad leaves and garnish with grapefruit segments. Drizzle over a little wine vinegar or lemon juice if liked.

Fried Rice with Hazel Nuts

Serves 4
Preparation 10 minutes, plus drying rice
Cooking time 15-18 minutes

	Metric	Imperial	American
Water	1.1 ltrs	2 pints	5 cups
Salt	2 tsp	2 tsp	2 tsp
Long grain rice	100 g	4 oz	¾ cup
Soya oil	4 tbsp	4 tbsp	4 tbsp
Hazelnuts (filberts)	225 g	8 oz	2 cups
Candied ginger (from a jar in syrup)	25 g	1 oz	1 oz
Candied angelica, diced	25 g	1 oz	1 oz
Cooked marrow peas	150 g	5 oz	¾ cup
Salt and black pepper			
Pancakes			
Eggs	3	3	3
Flour	1 tbsp	1 tbsp	1 tbsp
Water	6 tbsp	6 tbsp	6 tbsp
Chopped fresh parsley	1 tbsp	1 tbsp	1 tbsp

1 Bring the water to the boil with the salt and add the rice. Boil for 12 minutes, uncovered. Drain immediately in a colander and run hot or cold water over the rice to wash away the starch. Drain well again.

2 Spread the rice evenly over a large shallow tray. Refrigerate overnight. Stir occasionally to allow the rice to dry completely as moisture is evaporated under refrigerated conditions.

3 If you want to serve the rice on the same day, spread the rice on four baking trays. Roast in the oven at 180°C/350°F/gas mark 4 for 20 minutes, stirring from time to time to bring the moist grain to the top. A little oil can be sprinkled over to avoid sticking on the tray.

4 To prepare egg pancakes, beat the eggs in a bowl, add the flour, water and parsley. In a large pan heat 1 tbsp of the oil and add the egg mixture. Stir a little, cook flat without disturbing, toss on the other side and cook for 30 seconds more. Turn the pancake onto a pastry board. Roll it up and cut into shreds.

5 In the wok, heat the remaining oil and stir fry the hazelnuts for 1 minute. Add the candied ginger and angelica. Combine with the peas and 2 cups of the rice. Season to taste.

6 Mix the rice with the pancake strips and serve in small bowls. Serve the other heated plain fried rice separately. Garnish with spring onions.

— CHAPTER ELEVEN —

Celebration Desserts and Cakes

* *

You cannot have a celebration without a drink or special cake, gâteau or dessert to mark the happy event. Strawberry with Cointreau, Crêpes Suzette, Pears in red wine, Pineapple with Kirsch and Cherry Jubilee with ice cream will be very popular not forgetting the ubiquitous baked and flamed Alaska. Vegetarians are beginning to cut down on sugar intake and perhaps only as an exception for festive events might they indulge.

The clever cook knows you can reduce the amount of sugar in any recipe. Replacing jams by fruit purée can cut the sugar by sixty per cent and still be sweet enough. A yeast cake is less sweet than a sponge cake, so in this chapter I have tried to give you a selection of desserts and cakes most likely to please you — with the accent on less sugar and more fruity taste. Using sweet wines will cut the sugar in recipes. Pear or peach in sweet wines require no additional sugar. Dried fruit compote is sweet enough by itself. Using dried dates or figs also cuts down the amount of sugar needed. But a party is a party and to be enjoyed – for a spoonful of sugar helps the world to go round and brings a smile to happy faces!

Russian Fruit Kissel

Serves 4
Preparation 5 minutes
Cooking time 10 minutes

	Metric	Imperial	American
Cooking apples (Bramleys), cored, peeled and sliced	2	2	2
Fresh blackcurrants or blue berries, cleaned	150 g	5 oz	¾ cup
Water	150 ml	¼ pint	⅔ cup
Honey or granulated sugar	50 g	2 oz	2 oz
Juice and grated rind of lemon or lime	½	½	½
Pinch of ground cinnamon			
Single (light) cream	150 ml	¼ pint	⅔ cup
Potato starch or cornflour (cornstarch)	2 tbsp	2 tbsp	2 tbsp

1 Boil the apple slices and currants or berries in the water with the honey or sugar, lemon juice and rind and cinnamon for 5 minutes until soft. Pass the mixture through a nylon sieve to collect the purée. Reheat the purée until it begins to boil.

2 In a cup, mix the cream and starch and add to boiling purée. Cook for 4 minutes, then cool.

3 Serve cold in small bowls or glasses with wafers. Decorate with a few fresh currants or berries or frosted seedless grapes.

To frost grapes, lightly beat 2 egg whites. Dip grapes in the beaten whites, then in granulated sugar. Allow to dry for 2 hours at kitchen temperature. Cherries can also be frosted, as can other similar types of fruits with hard skins.

Variations
To make this fruit purée into an even more interesting dessert, add 12 g or 1 sachet of powered gelatine to the purée while still hot. When the purée is cool, fold in 1 cup whipped cream sweetened with 1 tbsp sugar. Flavour the mixture with 2 tbsp Kirsch or Cointreau. Pour into fancy glasses, chill for 1 hour and decorate with frosted grapes.

Both sweets can be served with macaroons or short-bread biscuits. Apples are the best base to use for all fruit purées.

A similar mixture can be made by using raspberries, strawberries or rhubarb instead of the blackcurrants or blueberries.

Italian Sabayon

Every good Italian restauranteur will offer you this warm wine custard in a large half pint glass, at the drop of a hat. It is light, alcoholic and still very much in favour. It is one of the most versatile, light and nourishing desserts and can be made with all kinds of sweet fortified wines, such as Marsala, Vermouth, Martini, Barsac, or sweet champagne like Asti Spumante.

Sabayon can be finished with any kind of spirits or liqueurs such as Cointreau, Grand Marnier, Kirsch or Cherry Brandy. It can be lightened with meringue or whipped cream when set, or served as a frozen dessert. Sabayon can also be served as a sauce for any kind of fruit compôte or fresh fruits such as pineapple, pear or figs.

Asti Spumante Sabayon

Serves 4
Preparation 4 minutes
Cooking time 4 minutes

	Metric	Imperial	American
Egg yolks	4	4	4
Caster (superfine) sugar	2-3 tbsp	2-3 tbsp	2-3 tbsp
Juice of lemon	½	½	½
Asti Spumante sparkling wine	225 ml	8 fl oz	1 cup
Cointreau	2 tbsp	2 tbsp	2 tbsp

1 Whisk the egg yolks, sugar, lemon juice and ½ cup of the wine in an electric mixer at full speed for 2 minutes.

2 Bring the remaining wine to the boil in a saucepan. Add it to the frothy mixture, whisking at a slow speed. Add the cointreau. Then increase the speed for another 2 minutes. The mixture should be thickish, frothy and over twice its original volume. Serve hot in dessert glasses. Decorate with frosted, seedless grapes.

Note:
For lasting thickness, place the bowl in a shallow tray half filled with water just under boiling and whisk by hand for 3 more minutes to ensure it will thicken. Do not exceed the temperature of 78°-80°C.

Fried Chinese Ice Cream

Serves 4
Preparation 10 minutes, plus freezing
Cooking time 2 minutes

All you need for this fun dessert is a good quality dairy ice cream made with eggs and real cream, some crumbs and oil for deep frying.

	Metric	Imperial	American
Scoops of dairy ice cream	8	8	8
Oil for deep frying			
Flour	6 tbsp	6 tbsp	6 tbsp
Eggs, beaten	2	2	2
White breadcrumbs	1 cup	1 cup	1 cup
Desiccated (shredded) coconut	1 tbsp	1 tbsp	1 tbsp

1 On a clean baking tray lined with greaseproof (wax) paper, place the scoops of ice cream. Refreeze immediately until really frozen — about 6 hours.

2 Heat the oil in a deep fryer to 190°C/375°F.

3 Coat each frozen scoop of ice cream all over in flour. Dust the surplus away. Dip in beaten egg, then roll in the breadcrumbs mixed with the coconut, making sure that there is a thick coating of crumbs and coconut.

4 Deep fry for 30 seconds only – this is very important. Serve immediately with a fruit coulis sauce of your choice.

Egg Custard Sauce for Rich Puddings

Serves 4
Preparation 5 minutes
Cooking time 10 minutes

Real egg custard is made with 6 egg yolks per 600 ml/ 1 pint/2½ cups milk used and 75 g/3 oz sugar. This is rather rich and very sweet and is made using the same procedure as Sabayon. Here is a much simpler custard using less sugar and fewer egg yolks.

	Metric	Imperial	American
Milk	600 ml	1 pint	2½ cups
Sugar	45 g	1½ oz	3 tbsp
Vanilla pod (bean)	1	1	1
Cornflour (cornstarch)	25 g	1 oz	¼ cup
Egg yolks	2	2	2
Brandy, rum or Grand Marnier	3 tbsp	3 tbsp	3 tbsp

1 Bring the milk to the boil with the sugar and vanilla pod.

2 In a cup mix the cornflour with 3 tbsp water. Add the blended cornflour to the boiling milk and stir. Cook for 3 minutes until it thickens slightly. Remove the vanilla pod.

3 In a small bowl mix the egg yolks and liqueur. Add ½ cup of the milk mixture, stirring. Pour the contents back into the thickened sauce. Reboil for 2 minutes.

4 Serve hot or cold for fruit compôtes or any kind of puddings, even with ice creams.

Note:
Instead of vanilla pod use vanilla essence, add at the last minute — 6 drops per 600 ml/1 pint/2½ cups.

Raspberry Coulis

Serves 4
Preparation 10 minutes
No cooking

This type of fruit sauce is used with any kind of frozen or cream desserts. It is less sweet than jam sauces and certainly more tasty. You can use other berries such as strawberries, blackberries, blueberries or any currants, red or black.

	Metric	Imperial	American
Fresh or frozen raspberries	225 g	8 oz	1¼ cups
Caster (superfine) sugar	75 g	3 oz	6 tbsp
Juice of lemon	½	½	½

1 Hull the raspberries, eliminating any bad ones. Wash quickly and drain on a tea towel.

2 Either liquidize all the ingredients to a soft purée or pass them through a nylon sieve (never metal as it discolours the fruit). Serve as an accompaniment to ice cream or other frozen desserts.

Apricot Coulis

Serves 4
Preparation 10 minutes
Cooking time about 4 minutes

This coulis can be made with other stone fruits, such as peaches, nectarines, plums. Use to accompany puddings, rice desserts, pancakes or fritters.

	Metric	Imperial	American
Fresh apricots	450 g	1 lb	1 lb
Sweet white wine or sweet sherry	150 ml	¼ pint	⅔ cup
Granulated sugar	50 g	2 oz	¼ cup
Kirsch or Cointreau	2 tbsp	2 tbsp	2 tbsp

1 Wash and drain the apricots. Remove the stones (pits).

2 Boil the apricots, wine and sugar until soft, about 4 minutes. Liquidize the mixture to a purée or pass through a nylon sieve. Lastly, add the Kirsch or Cointreau.

Strawberry Sorbet

Serves 6
Preparation 10 minutes, plus freezing
Cooking time 5 minutes

	Metric	Imperial	American
Fresh strawberries	225 g	8 oz	1½ cups
Icing (confectioner's) sugar	50 g	2 oz	½ cup
Caster (superfine) sugar	75 g	3 oz	6 tbsp
Egg white, from a very fresh egg	1	1	1
Juice of lemon	½	½	½
Grand Marnier	3 tbsp	3 tbsp	3 tbsp

1 Pick over the strawberries and discard any bad ones. Hull and cut into slices. Wash and drain. Retain some of the slices for garnish.

2 Liquidize the fruit and sugars to a purée. Add 100 ml/ 4 fl oz/scant ½ cup water. Bring to the boil in a stainless steel saucepan.

3 Meanwhile, in a bowl, whip the egg white with 1 tsp of sugar. Blend the meringue into the hot purée, whisking. Cook for 1 minute.

4 In a clean bowl, beat the mixture well. Add the lemon juice and liqueur.

5 Oil two ice cube trays with greaseproof (wax) paper and fill them with the mixture. Freeze for 2 hours. If the mixture crystalizes, whisk it again and refreeze. The meringue should stabilize the texture. Serve garnished with strawberries.

Autumn Fruit Pudding

Serves 4
Preparation 15 minutes, plus straining and chilling
Cooking time 5 minutes

With its abundance of berries and soft fruits, this delicious cold pudding is a favourite with children and teenagers. For the individual version which is far more attractive, you will need individual pudding basins, 220 ml/7 fl oz/1 cup capacity.

	Metric	Imperial	American
Slices of wholemeal bread	8	8	8
A selection of soft fruits, such as blackberries, blue berries, raspberries, currants or stoned cherries	750 g	1½ lb	1½ lb
Golden (corn) syrup or honey	2 tbsp	2 tbsp	2 tbsp
Red wine	100 ml	4 fl oz	½ cup
Powdered gelatine	1 tsp	1 tsp	1 tsp
Small glass of Kirsch	1	1	1

1 Line the base and sides of each pudding basin with bread.

2 Wash and drain all the fruits. Blend with the honey and wine and leave the fruits in a colander over a bowl to allow the juices to drip.

3 Fill the lined moulds with the fruit mixture. Boil the juice, then add and dissolve the gelatine. Pour this syrup and kirsch onto the fruit mixture. Cover each mould with a round of bread. Press tightly and chill.

4 Turn out onto plates and serve with yoghurt.

Apple and Rhubarb Mousse

Serves 4
Preparation 10 minutes, plus chilling
Cooking time 5-8 minutes

	Metric	Imperial	American
Bramley cooking apples, peeled, cored and sliced	225 g	8 oz	8 oz
Rhubarb sticks, peeled and cut in small pieces	150 g	6 oz	6 oz
Granulated sugar	150 g	6 oz	¾ cup
Powdered gelatine	10 g	⅓ oz	⅓ oz
Whipped cream	150 ml	¼ pint	⅔ cup

1 Boil the apple and rhubarb in a cupful of water until soft. Dissolve the sugar and gelatine in this mixture. Pass through a sieve to obtain a smooth purée or liquidize in a blender.

2 Fold in the whipped cream when the mixture is cold. Fill medium glasses. Chill until required. Serve with ratafia biscuits (see page 228).

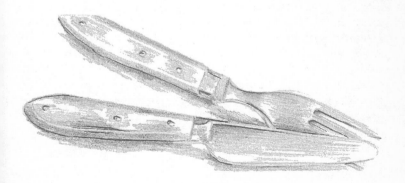

Caramelized Apple and Pear Tart

Serves 8
Preparation 15 minutes, plus resting
Cooking time 28 minutes

The feature of this tart is the caramelized effect which is produced at the first stage of cooking. The top of a gas cooker should be covered with asbestos to prevent the pan getting too hot and burning the caramel. An electric cooker top is best for this delicate operation.

	Metric	Imperial	American
Bramley apples, small sizes	225 g	8 oz	8 oz
Comice pears, ripe	225 g	8 oz	8 oz
Juice of lemon	1	1	1
Margarine	100 g	4 oz	½ cup
Granulated sugar	225 g	8 oz	1 cup
Flour for dusting			
Made puff pastry or shortcrust pastry	225 g	8 oz	8 oz

1 Peel, core and half all the fruits, then sprinkle with lemon juice. Place in the refrigerator in a shallow dish.

2 Smother the bottom of a shallow 20 cm/8 inch frying pan with unmelted margarine. Sprinkle the sugar over the margarine coating.

3 Arrange all the fruits in the pan with the cored cavities upwards.

4 Dust the pastry board with flour and roll a round of pastry to fit the area of the shallow round metal dish which can be used on the hob and in the oven. Trim the edges with a knife and remove surplus pastry. Rest the tart in a cool place for 30 minutes to prevent shrinking.

5 Place the pan on top of the cooker to caramelize the bottom of the pan for 8 minutes. Ensure an even cooking by lifting the edges of the pastry with a palette knife.

6 Bake in the oven at 225°C/425°F/gas mark 7 for another 20 minutes. Invert the tart onto a flat plate while still hot so that the pastry is underneath the fruits. Serve the tart piping hot with cream, flavoured with Kirsch or orange liqueur.

Normandy Apple Tart

Serves 8-10
Preparation 15 minutes, plus chilling
Cooking time 25-30 minutes

	Metric	Imperial	American
Sweet shortcrust pastry			
Self-raising flour	450 g	1 lb	4 cups
Ground cinnamon	1 tsp	1 tsp	1 tsp
Icing (confectioner's) sugar	25 g	1 oz	¼ cup
Butter	50 g	2 oz	¼ cup
Margarine	100 g	4 oz	½ cup
Eggs, beaten	2	2	2
Filling			
Butter	75 g	3 oz	6 tbsp
Granulated sugar	175 g	6 oz	¾ cup
Bramley cooking apples, cored, peeled and sliced	450 g	1 lb	1 lb
Cornflour (cornstarch)	3 tbsp	3 tbsp	3 tbsp
Water	6 tbsp	6 tbsp	6 tbsp
Icing (confectioner's) sugar, for dusting			

1 Brush an 27 cm×24 cm/11½ inch×9½ inch oblong baking tin with soft vegetable fat. Sift the flour, cinnamon and icing sugar onto a pastry board. Rub the butter and margarine into the flour mixture. Make a well in the centre and blend in the beaten eggs and 1-2 tbsp of water. Mix to a dough and knead lightly. Rest the dough and chill in the refrigerator for 1 hour.

2 In a shallow pan, melt the butter with the sugar and cook the apple slices for 5 minutes, stirring well.

3 In a cup, blend the cornflour and water and stir into the apple mixture to thicken the juice. (This is standard practice for any fruits to be used). Cook for 5 minutes and cool.

4 Divide the pastry into two pieces. On a floured board, roll out the pastry to an oblong 6 mm/¼ inch thick the same size as the tin. Wrap the pastry around the floured pin for easier lifting and unroll it over the greased baking tin. Prick the bottom all over with a fork. Part bake in the oven at 225°C/425°F/gas mark 7 for 8 minutes. Remove from the tin and cool.

5 When cold, spread the apple mixture over the baked pastry, leaving an edge around. Brush beaten egg all round and top up with another layer of pastry of the same thickness. Press the edges together to seal. Complete the baking of the tart at the same oven temperature for another 8-10 minutes until golden brown. Dust with icing sugar. Serve warm, cut into squares, with cream or egg custard.

Sweet Grapefruit Tart

Serves 8
Preparation 15 minutes
Cooking time 20 minutes

	Metric	Imperial	American
Shortcrust pastry	225 g	8 oz	8 oz
Filling			
Egg yolks	4	4	4
Caster (superfine) sugar	50 g	2 oz	4 tbsp
Juice of sweet grapefruit	1	1	1
Cornflour (cornstarch)	25 g	1 oz	2 tbsp
Cold water	2 tbsp	2 tbsp	2 tbsp
Sweet grapefruits	2	2	2
Grapefruit marmalade, warmed			

1 Roll out the pastry to a round on a floured pastry board to 6 mm/¼ inch thick to fit a 23 cm/9 inch tin, well greased with vegetable fat.

2 Place a piece of foil on the pastry base and fill with dry baking beans. Bake blind in the oven at 225°C/425°F/gas mark 7 for 8 minutes. Remove the foil and beans, then rebake for 5 minutes to dry the inside.

3 For the filling, in a metal bowl, whisk the egg yolks and sugar for 8 minutes. Boil the grapefruit juice in a small saucepan.

4 In a cup blend the cornflour and cold water. Add to the boiling grapefruit juice and cook for 4 minutes. Gradually add this hot liquid to the egg mixture, whisking. Reboil the filling for 3-4 minutes until it thickens like a custard.

5 Place the pastry case onto a flat dish. Fill the pastry with the cold grapefruit cream. Decorate with segments of grapefruit. Brush the top with hot melted grapefruit marmalade. Serve with lemon sorbet and cream.

Birthday Sponge Cake

Makes two 23 cm (9 inch) sponges
Preparation 10 minutes
Cooking time 20 minutes

To improve the whipping of the eggs, make sure the mixing bowl is clean and grease-free. Once the eggs and sugar have reached their peak, take care not to knock out air from the mixture or overmix when adding the flour. To vary the flavour, add cocoa powder by omitting the same amount of flour (15 g/½ oz per 150 g/5 oz flour).

If you use electric beaters, the eggs will take 8 minutes to fluff to the right consistency. Otherwise use a good balloon whisk.

For a jam filled sponge	Metric	Imperial	American
Eggs, beaten, about 4	150 g	5 oz	⅔ cup
Drops vanilla essence	6	6	6
Caster (superfine) sugar	300 g	10 oz	1¼ cups
Soft plain (all purpose) flour	300 g	10 oz	1¼ cups
Jam to fill			

1 Use two 23 cm/9 inch round cake tins, 5 cm/2 inches deep. Oil each tin carefully and line them with greaseproof (wax) paper. Oil the inside of the paper and dust with flour. Shake off the surplus flour by inverting the tins. Place a strip of greaseproof paper around the tins. Preheat the oven to 200°C/400°F/gas mark 6.

2 In a grease-free mixing bowl, whisk the eggs, vanilla and sugar for 8 minutes until it forms stiff peaks. Carefully and gradually blend in the sifted flour using a spatula or clean hands, until all the flour has been incorporated. The flour should be added in four lots and not all at once.

3 Divide the mixture between the prepared tins and level with a palette knife. Bake for 20 minutes until light and golden brown. Cool by inverting the tins over a wire rack.

4 When completely cold, slice in half horizontally and fill with apricot or sieved raspberry or strawberry jam. To make the jam spreading easier, whip the jam to pourable consistency. Alternatively, fill with whipped cream, or use half whipping and half double cream mixed, whipped together until it holds in the whisk.

	Metric	Imperial	American
For a Marzipan and Icing Topped Sponge			
Apricot jam	75 g	3 oz	¼-⅓ cup
Icing (confectioner's) sugar for dusting	50 g	2 oz	½ cup
Marzipan (almond paste)	225 g	8 oz	8 oz
Icing (confectioner's) sugar, sifted	225 g	8 oz	2 cups
Egg white, stirred	1	1	1
Food colour as required			

1 To marzipan the sponge, first cut the top of the sponge level if it is dome shaped, using a bread knife. The top part must be flat.

2 Heat the apricot jam to boiling point and brush it over the top and sides of the sponge (using it to stick the marzipan).

3 Dust icing sugar on a pastry board and roll out the marzipan to a thickness of 4 mm/⅙ inch. Lay the round on top of the sponge.

4 Cut strips of marzipan to the same width as the sides of the sponge. For easier application, roll up the marzipan strip, then unroll it as you apply this band to the side of the sponge.

5 For the icing, beat the sifted icing sugar and egg white in a clean metal bowl. To obtain a good consistency, heat the bowl over a saucepan of boiling water. The mixture should be spreadable without being too stiff or liquid.

6 Reserve half a cup of the icing to be coloured for any writing or decoration. Add drops of colour, pale blue for boys or pale pink for girls and chocolate for adults. Stir the icing mixture using a palette knife until even. Leave to dry a little.

7 Using a small 2 mm tube (tip) in a piping bag, pipe the name or inscription on the cake or on a rectangle of marzipan which can be placed on top of the cake.

Note:
The plain sponge is suitable for trifles and many other desserts.

Swedish Raisin Sour Cake

Serves 8
Preparation 10 minutes
Cooking time 35 minutes

This is a delicious flan made with sour cream and seed-less raisins. It is eaten at midnight in Sweden on Midsummer's Eve.

	Metric	Imperial	American
Shortcrust pastry	225 g	8 oz	8 oz
Filling			
Flour	2 tbsp	2 tbsp	2 tbsp
Eggs, beaten	2	2	2
Caster (superfine) sugar	4 tbsp	4 tbsp	4 tbsp
Sour cream	250 ml	8 fl oz	1 cup
Seedless raisins	225 g	8 oz	1⅓ cups
Rum or brandy	4 tbsp	4 tbsp	4 tbsp
Drops vanilla essence (extract)	2	2	2
Drops lemon essence	3	3	3

1 Oil a flan tin, 23 cm/9 inches in diameter. Line it with a round of pastry, 0.5 cm/¼ inch thick.

2 In a bowl, mix the flour, eggs, sugar and cream to a batter. Add the seedless raisins, rum and essences.

3 Fill the pastry case with the mixture. Bake in the oven at 200°C/400°F/gas mark 6 for 20 minutes. Reduce the heat to 180°C/350°F/gas mark 4 and cook for 5 minutes until baked like a custard.

Trifle Treasure

Serves 8
Preparation 10 minutes, plus setting
Cooking time 5 minutes

Jelly and custard trifles are more popular than the old fashioned sherry kind so favoured by our Victorian ancestors. The more modern version presented in Nouvelle Cuisine style is certainly more attractive as the trifle is unmoulded onto a plate, without too much cream decoration. It is even more attractive to set the trifle in individual glass bowls.

	Metric	Imperial	American
Sponge base (see page 218)	1	1	1
Raspberry jam	75 g	3 oz	⅓ cup
Raspberry jelly (flavoured gelatin)	150 g	5 oz	5 oz
Fresh or frozen raspberries, sieved	150 g	6 oz	1 cup
Custard			
Custard powder	25 g	1 oz	2 tbsp
Caster (superfine) sugar	50 g	2 oz	¼ cup
Milk	300 ml	½ pint	1¼ cups
Decoration			
Fresh raspberries	225 g	8 oz	1 cup
Oranges, peeled and cut into segments	2	2	2
Whipped cream	150 ml	¼ pint	⅔ cup
Caster (superfine) sugar	25 g	1 oz	2 tbsp
Grated or fancy chocolate sweet			

1 Split the sponge into two halves and fill with jam. Cut into small cubes.

2 To prepare the raspberry jelly, dissolve it in 600 ml/ 1 pint/2½ cups boiling water. Cool a little and pour 2 tbsp of the jelly into eight pyrex 150 ml/¼ pint/⅔ cup capacity moulds. Set the moulds in the refrigerator.

3 Divide the sponge cubes between the moulds and soak with the remaining liquid raspberry jelly mixture and sieved raspberries.

4 To prepare the custard, in a cup mix the custard powder and sugar with a little cold milk. Boil the rest of the milk. Add the mixture and cook for 4 minutes until thick and smooth, stirring.

5 Top up the moulds with this custard and chill.

6 Turn the moulded trifles onto eight plates. Decorate with fresh raspberries and orange segments. Pipe a little cream on top and sprinkle with grated chocolate or use a chocolate sweet.

Chocolate Bar with Toasted Almonds

Serves 4
Preparation 15 minutes, plus setting
Cooking time 10 minutes

	Metric	Imperial	American
Dark chocolate, grated or cut in small pieces	150 g	6 oz	6 oz
Milk	100 ml	4 fl oz	½ cup
Powdered gelatine	10 g	⅓ oz	⅓ oz
Eggs, separated	3	3	3
Double (heavy) cream	100 ml	4 fl oz	½ cup
Caster (superfine) sugar	3 tbsp	3 tbsp	3 tbsp
Toasted flaked almonds, to decorate	3 tbsp	3 tbsp	3 tbsp
Raspberries or poached pear slices (optional)			

1 Line a 600 ml/1 pint/2½ cup loaf tin (pan) with greaseproof (wax) paper.

2 Place the chocolate pieces to melt in a large mixing bowl (preferably stainless steel), over a saucepan of boiling water.

3 Boil the milk and dissolve the gelatine.

4 Add the egg yolks to the melted chocolate. Stir in the hot milk mixture well, then the cream.

5 Beat the egg whites to a meringue. Add the sugar then, when stiff, fold into the chocolate mixture.

6 Fill the prepared oblong mould and chill for 3 hours until set. To serve, unmould and cut into thick slices, dipping a knife into boiling water for a neat cut. Place on individual plates and decorate with the almonds. Accompany with fresh raspberries or poached pears if liked.

Ratafia Biscuits

Makes 16 biscuits
Preparation 15 minutes
Cooking time 15 minutes

	Metric	Imperial	American
Granulated sugar	100 g	4 oz	½ cup
Ground almonds	50 g	2 oz	½ cup
Ground rice	½ tbsp	½ tbsp	½ tbsp
Egg white	50 ml	2 oz	1
Almonds, split	25 g	1 oz	2 tbsp
Apricot jam, boiled			

1 Well oil and flour a 30 cm/12 inch baking tin. Line with rice paper. Use rice paper and no other as it is edible.

2 In a bowl blend together the sugar, almonds and ground rice, then beat in the egg white for 2 minutes.

3 Using a 5 mm/¼ inch plain tube (tip) and piping bag, pipe the ratafia mixture onto the prepared baking tin into button-sized biscuits 1 cm/½ inch diameter, or in the shape of a pear or cat's tail. Place one split almond on top of each biscuit.

4 Bake in the oven at 190°C/375°F/gas mark 5 for 15 minutes until golden in colour. Sandwich together two biscuits with boiled apricot jam.

Sherry Syllabub

Serves 8
Preparation 8 minutes
No cooking

This delicate sherry cream dessert was famed long ago at the time of Charles II as the perfect sweet for sweethearts.

	Metric	Imperial	American
Double (heavy) cream	300 ml	½ pint	1¼ cups
Grated zest and juice of lemon	1	1	1
Medium sherry	50 ml	2 fl oz	¼ cup
Grand Marnier liqueur	50 ml	2 fl oz	¼ cup
Ratafia biscuits	8	8	8

1 In a bowl, whisk the cream until stiff. Blend in lightly the sugar, lemon, sherry and Grand Marnier.

2 Half fill stemmed glasses with this mixture and decorate with ratafia biscuits or fresh strawberries when in season.

Crêpes de Noel

Serves 6
Preparation 8 minutes, plus resting
Cooking time 6-8 minutes

All pancakes should be very thin, for this reason it is best to use half milk and water rather than milk only to produce a thin batter.

	Metric	Imperial	American
Pancake batter			
Plain flour	150 g	5 oz	1¼ cups
Buckwheat flour	150 g	5 oz	1¼ cups
Icing (confectioner's) sugar, sifted	25 g	1 oz	¼ cup
Salt	¼ tsp	¼ tsp	¼ tsp
Eggs, beaten	3	3	3
Milk	175 ml	6 fl oz	¾ cup
Water or beer	175 ml	6 fl oz	¾ cup
Rum	1 tbsp	1 tbsp	1 tbsp
Oil	2 tbsp	2 tbsp	2 tbsp
Granulated sugar for sprinkling			

1 In a bowl, combine all the dry ingredients and rub well to a crumble. Add the beaten eggs, milk, water or beer, rum and oil. Leave to rest for 2 hours.

2 Use a small omelette pan 15 cm/6 inches diameter, to produce two pancakes per portion. Alternatively, use a 20 cm/8 inch pan to produce one large pancake per portion.

3 Grease the pan with a teaspoon of oil per pancake. Heat the pan with the oil and pour in 50 ml/2 fl oz of batter when the pan is very hot. Cook for 30 seconds on each side. Toss and spread on a try lined with greaseproof (wax) paper, sprinkled with granulated sugar.

4 Serve with a wedge of lemon, your favourite jam, a mixture of fresh strawberries and bananas or fruit mincemeat.

5 For fruit mincemeat. Blend together 1 tbsp each of the following fruits: seedless raisins, sultanas (golden raisins), chopped dates, grated apple, and grated lemon and juice. Heat 2 tbsp of butter and sugar together, then blend in the fruits. Flavour with 1 tsp mixed spices.

New Year Tipsy Sponge Savarins

Serves 6
Preparation 20 minutes, plus rising
Cooking time 20 minutes

	Metric	Imperial	American
Yeast Batter Mixture			
Strong bread flour, sifted	225 g	8 oz	2 cups
Milk, tepid	50 ml	2 fl oz	¼ cup
Dry yeast	1 tsp	1 tsp	1 tsp
Icing (confectioner's) sugar	1 tsp	1 tsp	1 tsp
Flour	1 tsp	1 tsp	1 tsp
Eggs, beaten	2	2	2
Butter, melted	100 g	4 oz	½ cup
Syrup			
Water	225 ml	8 fl oz	1¼ cups
Sugar	175 ml	6 oz	¾ cup
Teabag	1	1	1
Kirsch	4 tbsp	4 tbsp	4 tbsp
Decoration			
Black cherries, stoned	225 g	8 oz	1 cup
Red wine	100 ml	4 fl oz	½ cup
Sugar	25 g	1 oz	2 tbsp
Ground cinnamon	1 tsp	1 tsp	1 tsp
Cornflour (cornstarch)	1 tsp	1 tsp	1 tsp
Water	3 tbsp	3 tbsp	3 tbsp

1 For the yeast batter, in a bowl place the sifted flour and make a well in the centre. In a cup mix the dry yeast with the tepid milk, icing sugar and flour to produce a ferment. Pour this into the well of flour and leave to ferment for 15 minutes until it begins to froth.

Vegetab

2 Mix the ingredients with the beaten eggs to a soft dough. Cover with a cloth or polythene sheet and allow to rise for 1 hour.

3 Knead the butter into the dough until smooth. Rest for 15 minutes. You need six small savarin metal ring moulds, well oiled and dusted with flour. Half fill each mould with the yeast dough mixture. Allow to prove until double in size. Bake in the oven at 200°C/400°F/gas mark 6 for 15-20 minutes until golden. Unmould and cool on a wire rack.

4 For the syrup, boil the water and sugar for 2 minutes. Remove from the heat and add the tea bag. Leave for 8 minutes, then remove the tea bag. Flavour with Kirsch. Pour the hot syrup into a tray. Soak each ring in hot syrup, then carefully remove with a flat slice or spatula. Place the rings onto plates.

5 For the filling, boil the cherries, wine, sugar and cinnamon for 2 minutes. Mix the cornflour and water and add to the cherries. Cook for 4 minutes to thicken and clear the starch. Fill each ring with cherries. Serve cream separately.

Passion Fruit Soufflés

Serves 6
Preparation 15 minutes
Cooking time 20 minutes

	Metric	Imperial	American
Ripe bananas, peeled and puréed	4	4	4
Passion fruits	6	6	6
Egg yolks	3	3	3
Rum	3 tbsp	3 tbsp	3 tbsp
Double (heavy) cream	4 tbsp	4 tbsp	4 tbsp
Egg whites	6	6	6
Caster (superfine) sugar	75 g	3 oz	6 tbsp
Sauce			
Apricot jam	3 tbsp	3 tbsp	3 tbsp
Rum	3 tbsp	3 tbsp	3 tbsp
Garnish			
Banana, sliced	3	3	3

1 Pass the banana through a moulinette or a sieve. Collect the pulp from the passion fruits and mix it with the banana purée.

2 Blend the purée in a bowl with the egg yolks, rum and cream.

3 In a mixing bowl, beat the egg white until it holds to the whisk but is not too firm. At this stage add the sugar, a little at a time. Mix one third of this meringue with the banana mixture. Beat thoroughly. Fold in the remaining meringue very lightly.

4 Well butter six ovenproof soufflé ramekins, 225 ml/ 8 fl oz/1 cup capacity. Dust with caster sugar inside and place on a baking tray ready for baking at the last moment. Fill each soufflé mould to the brim. Make a circle with the back of a teaspoon to form a groove, detaching the mixture from the side of each mould, this will help in even rising. Bake in the oven at 200°C/400°F/gas mark 6 for about 20 minutes until well risen.

5 Meanwhile, warm the apricot jam and rum. Add the sieved bananas. Serve the soufflés immediately accompanied with the sliced bananas.

Gâteau de Nouvel An

Serves 8
Preparation 10 minutes
Cooking time 45-50 minutes

This type of cake is very popular to serve to guests with a glass of sherry as they arrive for a New Year party. The basis of the recipe can be adapted on the principle of the same weight of flour, butter and sugar and an equivalent weight of eggs.

Round, oval or square tins may be used for this cake, even a heart shape for certain celebrations.

	Metric	Imperial	American
Butter	100 g	4 oz	½ cup
Caster (superfine) sugar	100 g	4 oz	½ cup
Large eggs, beaten	2	2	2
Flour, soft	75 g	3 oz	⅔ cup
Desiccated (shredded) coconut	3 tbsp	3 tbsp	3 tbsp
Rum	2 tbsp	2 tbsp	2 tbsp
Drops of almond essence (extract)	2	2	2
Drops of lemon essence (extract)	2	2	2
Drops of vanilla essence (extract)	2	2	2

1 In a bowl, cream the butter and sugar until fluffy. Add the eggs gradually, then fold in the flour and coconut gently. Flavour with rum.

2 Oil a 15 cm/6 inch diameter, 6.5 cm/2 inch deep cake tin and line with greaseproof (wax) paper. Oil again and dust with flour. Fill the tin with the mixture almost to the brim. Level the top with the back of your hand or a spoon.

3 Bake in the oven at 190°C/375°F/gas mark 5 for 45-50 minutes. To check, insert a fine skewer, if it comes out clean and dry, the cake is cooked, if mixture adheres to it, leave to bake for another 10 minutes or so.

4 Invert tin onto a wire rack and cool, only unmould when the cake is cold. Leave overnight before serving.

Celebration Cake

Serves 10
Preparation 15 minutes
Cooking time 1 hour 50 minutes

	Metric	Imperial	American
Soft butter or margarine, or mixture of both	100 g	4 oz	½ cup
Dark brown sugar	100 g	4 oz	½ cup
Large eggs, beaten	4	4	4
Glycerine	2 tsp	2 tsp	2 tsp
Plain (all purpose) flour	150 g	5 oz	1¼ cups
Ground almonds	25 g	1 oz	¼ cup
Baking powder	½ tsp	½ tsp	½ tsp
Ground mixed spices	½ tsp	½ tsp	½ tsp
Ground cinnamon	¼ tsp	¼ tsp	¼ tsp
Currants	100 g	4 oz	⅔ cup
Sultanas (golden raisins)	100 g	4 oz	⅔ cup
Seedless raisins	100 g	4 oz	⅔ cup
Mixed candied peel	25 g	1 oz	2 tbsp
Glacé (candied) cherries	25 g	1 oz	2 tbsp
Walnuts	25 g	1 oz	2 tbsp
Rum	1 tbsp	1 tbsp	1 tbsp
Grated rind of lemon and orange	1 tsp	1 tsp	1 tsp
Drops vanilla essence (extract)	3	3	3
Drops lemon essence (extract)	3	3	3
Drops almond essence (extract)	2	2	2

1 In a mixing bowl, cream the butter and sugar for 6 minutes until light and fluffy. Gradually add the egg mixture, beating continually. Avoid curdling.

2 Carefully blend in the glycerine which will help keep the cake moist after baking.

3 Sift the flour, ground almonds, baking powder and spices. Blend lightly into the butter mixture without beating.

4 Combine the fruits in a bowl with 1 tbsp of flour. Add the nuts, rum, grated rind and all the essences. Blend the fruit lightly into the cake mixture to disperse it thoroughly.

5 Well oil a 15 or 20 cm/6 or 8 inch deep cake tin. Dust with flour and line with double greaseproof (wax) paper. Fill the prepared tin to the top and level the mixture with the back of your hand slightly dampened. Cover with foil during baking to prevent browning too much. Remove after 1 hour.

6 Bake in the oven at 180°C/350°F/gas mark 4 for 1 hour 50 minutes. If the surface of the cake bounces back when pressed, then it is ready. Alternatively, insert a fine skewer which should be clean and dry when removed.

7 When baked, remove from the tin and cool on a wire rack. The cake must be cold before attempting to cover with marzipan paste (see page 221). Ice and decorate as liked.

Note
Very good books on cake decorations will show you the technique for royal icing coating, decorating and piping.

Festive Austrian Stollen

Makes 3 loaves
Preparation 15 minutes, plus rising
Cooking time 30 minutes

This is the ideal yeast cake for Christmas and New Year parties.

	Metric	Imperial	American
For the dough			
Fresh yeast	1 tbsp	1 tbsp	1 tbsp
Water warm at 28°C/80°F	100 ml	4 fl oz	½ cup
Strong flour	25 g	1 oz	¼ cup
Sugar	1 tbsp	1 tbsp	1 tbsp
For the fruit dough			
Egg, beaten	1	1	1
Demerara sugar	75 g	3 oz	½ cup
Salt	1 tsp	1 tsp	1 tsp
Strong bread flour	450 g	1 lb	4 cups
Ground almonds	50 g	2 oz	½ cup
Ground cinnamon	1 tsp	1 tsp	1 tsp
Seedless raisins	225 g	8 oz	1⅓ cups
Mixed candied peel	50 g	2 oz	⅓ cup
Rum	2 tbsp	2 tbsp	2 tbsp
Butter, melted	100 g	4 oz	½ cup
For the filling and glaze			
Marzipan (almond paste)	175 g	6 oz	6 oz
Egg, beaten	1	1	1
Sugar	6 tbsp	6 tbsp	6 tbsp
Water	6 tbsp	6 tbsp	6 tbsp
Flaked almonds	50 g	2 oz	½ cup
Icing (confectioner's) sugar, for dusting			

1 Dissolve the yeast in the warm water and add the other ingredients. Leave to ferment for 30 minutes until it froths.

2 To this fermented mixture add the egg, sugar, salt and flour. Mix to a smooth elastic dough. Add the spice, raisins, peel and rum and mix well. Rest for 30 minutes.

3 Divide the dough into three, shape into rounds and roll out each flat like pastry. Spread a little butter over the top.

4 Roll the marzipan into a roll 2 cm/¾ inch in diameter like a sausage. Place a stick of it in the middle of each flat round. Fold over the edges of each one and press down in the centre. Put each loaf on a well oiled 30 cm/12 inch baking tray.

5 Brush with egg and cover with a polythene bag to prove for about 40 minutes until double in size. Bake in the oven at 220°C/425°F/gas mark 7 for 30 minutes until golden brown.

6 Meanwhile, boil the sugar in 6 tbsp water for 3 minutes to make a syrup. When baked, brush syrup over each loaf and sprinkle the top with flaked almonds and icing sugar. Serve with a glass of Madeira wine or white port.

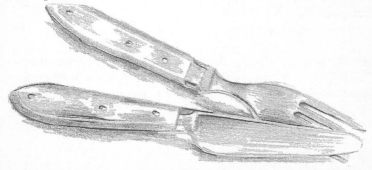

Conil Cheese Cake

Serves 8
Preparation 25 minutes, plus chilling
No cooking

This is another of my baker son's special favourite desserts.

	Metric	Imperial	American
Base			
Unsalted butter	50 g	2 oz	¼ cup
Digestive biscuits (Graham crackers), crumbled	100 g	4 oz	½ cup
Sesame seeds	2 tbsp	2 tbsp	2 tbsp
Fresh strawberries halved or sliced	150 g	6 oz	1 cup
Filling			
Curd or cream cheese	225 g	8 oz	1 cup
Lemon curd	2 tbsp	2 tbsp	2 tbsp
Lemon juice	3 tbsp	3 tbsp	3 tbsp
Caster (superfine) sugar	2 tbsp	2 tbsp	2 tbsp
Powdered gelatine	2 tbsp	2 tbsp	2 tbsp
Water	50 ml	2 fl oz	¼ cup
Whipping cream	175 ml	6 fl oz	¾ cup
Stoned cherries (Morello)	50 g	2 oz	2 oz
Cherry brandy	2 tbsp	2 tbsp	2 tbsp

Garnish
Toasted flaked almonds

1 Use a collapsible bottom round cake tin 5 cm/2 inches deep and 20 cm/8 inches in diameter. Oil the base and line the edges with a strip or band of greaseproof (wax) paper.

2 For the base, melt the butter and mix with the crushed biscuit crumbs and sesame seeds. Press the mixture into the bottom of the prepared tin. Arrange a row of sliced strawberries over the biscuit base. The remaining strawberries should be kept to decorate the finished cheesecake.

3 In a bowl, blend together the cheese, curd, lemon juice and sugar.

4 Dissolve the gelatine in hot water and add to the cheese mixture.

5 Whip the cream and fold it into the mixture. Add the cherries and brandy.

6 Fill the cake tin and chill for 6 hours until set.

7 Before serving, decorate the top with strawberries. Cut into wedges to serve. Finish with a sprinkling of toasted flaked almonds. Serve with cream or ice cream.

Note:
The digestive biscuits should be placed in a cloth or plastic bag and crushed with a rolling pin. After crushing they may be sieved to give a finer texture to the base.

Celebration Pecan Pie

Serves 6
Preparation 10 minutes
Cooking time 30 minutes

	Metric	Imperial	American
Shortcrust pastry (basic pie dough)	225 g	8 oz	8 oz
Filling			
Flour	2 tbsp	2 tbsp	2 tbsp
Brown sugar	100 g	4 oz	½ cup
Eggs, beaten	3	3	3
Salt			
Butter	100 g	4 oz	½ cup
Maple syrup and honey	225 g	8 oz	⅔ cup
Pecan nuts, chopped	225 g	8 oz	1⅓ cups
Drops vanilla essence (extract)	6	6	6

1 Line a well oiled 20 cm/8 inch tart tin with the pastry.

2 In a bowl, mix the flour and sugar. Add the eggs, salt, butter, syrup and honey, nuts and vanilla essence.

3 Fill the pastry case with the mixture. Bake in the oven at 190°C/375°F/gas mark 5 for the first 10 minutes, then reduce the temperature to 180°C/350°F/gas mark 4 for a further 20 minutes. Serve with whipped cream or dairy ice cream with a compôte of plums or apricots.

Apple and Apricot Fritters

Serves 6
Preparation 10 minutes
Cooking time 5-8 minutes

There is no better way to enjoy fruits than fried in batter, using unsaturated oil as a frying medium.

	Metric	Imperial	American
Large Bramley or any cooking apples, peeled, cored and cut into rings	2	2	2
Oil for deep frying			
Apricots, stoned (pitted)	6	6	6
Flour for dusting	2 tbsp	2 tbsp	2 tbsp
Ground cinnamon	1 tbsp	1 tbsp	1 tbsp
Pancake batter (page 230)	600 ml	1 pint	2½ cups
Granulated sugar, for sprinkling			

1 Heat the oil in a deep fryer.

2 Coat apple rings and apricots in a mixture of flour and cinnamon.

3 Dip each one in batter and fry for 1-2 minutes until golden brown. Drain on absorbent paper and sprinkle with granulated sugar. Serve with apricot coulis (see page 207).

INDEX

almonds
  asparagus mousse with
  toasted almonds 51-52
  chocolate bar with toasted
  almonds 226-227
  courge aux amandes 77-78
  gratin des deux pommes aux
  amandes 174-175
  leek and almond
  cream 147-148
  nutty white sauce 28
apples
  apple and apricot
  fritters 248
  apple and beetroot wine
  soup 18-19
  apple and rhubarb
  mousse 211
  caramelized apple and pear
  tart 212-213
  gratin des deux pommes aux
  amandes 174-175
  Normandy apple
  tart 214-215
apricots
  apple and apricot
  fritters 248
  apricot coulis 207
artichokes
  artichoke, cucumber and
  potato flash 178-179
  Jerusalem artichoke
  sauté 79
asparagus
  asparagus, bean shoots
  and red bean
  assortment 194-195
  asparagus mousse with
  toasted almonds 51-52
  French asparagus soufflé
  omelette 136-137
  pan fried asparagus and egg
  cutlets 98-99
Asti Spumante sabayon 203
aubergines
  aubergine caviar 40
  baked timbale
  d'aubergine 85-86
  caponata à la
  Conil 90-91
  lasagna verdi aux
  aubergines 103-104
  tofu medley of aubergine,

  potato and
  celeriac 192-193
Austrian stollen,
  festive 242-243
autumn fruit pudding 210
avocados
  avocado and rice bean
  salad 60-61
  avocado and tomato
  soup 14
bananas, passion fruit
  soufflés 235-236
beans see pulses
beer 37
  beer soup with sweet
  onion 22
beetroot, apple and beetroot
  wine soup 18-19
broccoli
  broccoli beignets 87-88
  broccoli and button
  mushrooms 186-187
  broccoli and tomato
  quiche 138-139
Brussels sprouts, button
  sprouts, chestnuts and new
  potatoes 182-183
cabbage, coleslaw with
  pineapple and cashew
  nuts 65-66
cakes see desserts and cakes
carrots
  broad beans and carrot
  custard pie 146-147
  carrot and spinach tofu
  cakes 94-95
  carrot and yoghurt pâté
  dip 43
  peacock feather fan of
  carrots and
  cucumber 62-63
cashew nuts, coleslaw
  with pineapple and
  cashew nuts 65-66
cauliflower, pickled cauliflower
  salad 71-72
celebration cake 239-241
celebration pecan pie 246
celeriac, tofu medley of
  aubergine, potato and
  celeriac 192-193
champagne 37

cheese
  cheese sauce 27
  Chinese cocktail
  rolls 96-97
  Conil cheese cake 244-245
  courgette Swiss
  rarebit 80-81
  cream cheese bonne
  bouche 76
  cream cheese and leek
  dip 50
  gratin des deux pommes
  aux amandes 174-175
  Greek cheese and spinach
  pie 140-141
  hot cheese and potato pâté
  with herbs 42
  Indian chickpeas and fried
  cheese dumplings 162-163
  poached egg
  Florentine 145-146
  pomme farcie au fromage
  blanc 171
  sesame cheesecake 92-93
  tartlets de petits pois et
  fromage purée 88-89
chestnuts
  button sprouts, chestnuts
  and new potatoes 182-183
  pilaf aux châtaignes 117
chickpeas
  chickpea and spinach
  casserole 154
  hummus (chickpea caviar) 41
  Indian chickpeas and fried
  cheese dumplings 162-163
chicory
  chicory with potato
  salad 66-67
  lentil cakes with
  chicory 160-161
Chinese dishes
  asparagus, bean shoots and
  red bean
  assortment 194-195
  broccoli and button
  mushrooms 186-187
  Chinese cocktail
  rolls 96-97
  Chinese omelette 134
  Chinese rainbow of
  peppers 190-191
  fried rice with hazel
  nuts 196-197
  jardinière de légumes
  Cantonese style 188-189
  tofu medley of aubergine,
  potato and
  celeriac 192-193
chocolate bar with toasted
  almonds 226-227
cider 37
citrus fruits
  citrus fruits on spinach and
  bean sprouts 68-69
  see also named fruit
coconuts
  coconut sauce 28
  fried coconut cream
  delight 143-144
coleslaw with pineapple and
  cashew nuts 65-66
courgettes
  caponata à la Conil 90-91
  courgette pasta salad in
  basil sauce 59-60
  courgette Swiss
  rarebit 80-81
crêpes
  crêpes aux
  poireaux 110-111
  crêpes de Noel 230-231
  egg bretone 137
cucumber
  artichoke, cucumber and
  potato flash 178-179
  cucumber and mint in
  yoghurt dressing 74
  peacock feather fan of
  carrots and
  cucumber 62-63
  tomato and cucumber in
  brandy dressing 58-59
custard, egg custard sauce for
  rich puddings 205-206
dairy white sauce 27
desserts and cakes
  apple and apricot
  fritters 248
  apple and rhubarb
  mousse 211
  apricot coulis 207
  Asti Spumante
  sabayon 203
  autumn fruit pudding 210
  birthday sponge
  cake 218-221
  caramelized apple and pear
  tart 212-213
  celebration cake 239-241
  celebration pecan pie 246
  chocolate bar with toasted
  almonds 226-227
  Conil cheese cake 244-245

crêpes de Noel 230–231
egg custard sauce for rich
  puddings 205–206
festive Austrian
  stollen 242–243
fried Chinese ice
  cream 204
gâteau de Nouvel
  An 237–238
Italian sabayon 202–203
New Year tipsy sponge
  savarins 232–234
Normandy apple
  tart 214–215
passion fruit
  soufflés 235–236
raspberry coulis 206
ratafia biscuits 228
Russian fruit
  kissel 200–201
sherry syllabub 229
strawberry sorbet 208
Swedish raisin sour
  cake 222
sweet grapefruit
  tart 216–217
trifle treasure 224–225
dips
  African peanut queen
    dip 46
  carrot and yoghurt pâté
    dip 43
  cream cheese and leek
    dip 50
  pine and basil pistou
    provencal dip 47
drinks 37
eggplants see aubergines
eggs
  baked timbale
    d'aubergine 85–86
  broad beans and carrot
    custard pie 146–147
  broccoli and tomato
    quiche 138–139
  Chinese omelette 134
  egg bretonne 137
  egg custard sauce for rich
    puddings 205–206
  egg sauce 27
  French asparagus soufflé
    omelette 136–137
  fried coconut cream
    delight 143–144
  Greek cheese and spinach
    pie 140–141
  Italian style

frittata 132–133
leek and almond
  cream 147–148
pain perdu 135
pan fried asparagus and egg
  cutlets 98–99
poached egg
  Florentine 145–146
poached egg Turkish
  style 130
shredded omelette Japanese
  style 131
tarte de tomates et haricots
  verts nicoise 142–143
timbale de riz
  parisienne 121
tomato piperade 82–83
fennel, bean sprouts and
  fennel with egg
  noodles 166–167
fruit
  autumn fruit pudding 210
  passion fruit
    soufflés 235–236
  pawpaw pecan
    cocktail 54–55
  Russian fruit
    kissel 200–201
  see also named fruit
garbanzo beans see
  chickpeas
garlic soup of
  Provence 20–21
gâteau de Nouvel
  An 237–238
gazpacho with chilli,
  Mexican 17
gnocchi, polenta gnocchi with
  walnuts 106–107
goulash of potato and onion
  in paprika sauce 177–178
grapefruits
  citrus fruits on spinach and
    bean sprouts 68–69
  sweet grapefruit
    tart 216–217
hazel nuts, fried rice
  with 196–197
hummus (chickpea caviar) 41
ice cream, fried Chinese 204
Italian sabayon 202–203
kedgeree, Indian 125
lasagna verdi aux
  aubergines 103–104
leeks
  cream cheese and leek
    dip 50

crêpes aux
poireaux 110-111
leek and almond
cream 147-148
lemons
citrus fruits on spinach and
bean sprouts 68-69
lemon and egg soup 15
lemon sauce 33
lentils *see* pulses
light meals
baked timbale
d'aubergine 85-86
broccoli beignets 87-88
caponata à la Conil 90-91
carrot and spinach tofu
cakes 94-95
Chinese cocktail
rolls 96-97
courge aux amandes 77-78
courgette Swiss
rarebit 80-81
cream cheese bonne
bouche 76
Jerusalem artichoke
sauté 79
onions stuffed with
mushrooms and olives 83-84
pan fried asparagus and egg
cutlets 98-99
sesame cheesecake 92-93
tartlets de petits pois et
fromage purée 88-89
tomato piperade 82-83
limes, citrus fruits on spinach
and bean sprouts 68-69
Macedoine flan 114-115
Madeira 37
Madeira sauce 30
marrows
courge aux amandes 77-78
courge aux
flageolets 164-165
courge aux pommes
savoyarde 175-176
mayonnaise 34-5
mint
cucumber and mint in
yoghurt dressing 74
mint sauce 35
mushrooms
broccoli and button
mushrooms 186-187
hot mushroom salad 73
mushroom and pepper
moulds 55-56
mushroom

sauce 27, 28, 29
onions stuffed with
mushrooms and olives 83-84
tarte de champignons in
brandy sauce 112-113
terrine de légumes aux
champignons blancs 156-157
timbale de riz parisienne 121
New Year tipsy sponge
savarins 232-234
Normandy apple tart 214-215
nuts
nutty brown sauce 29-30
nutty white sauce 28
see also individual nut
varieties
okra, caponata à la
Conil 90-91
olives
green olive pâté 53-54
olive sauce 30
onions stuffed with
mushrooms and olives 83-84
omelettes
Chinese omelette 134
French asparagus soufflé
omelette 136-137
Italian style
frittata 132-133
shredded omelette Japanese
style 131
onions
beer soup with sweet
onion 22
goulash of potato and onion
in paprika sauce 177-178
onion sauce 27
onions stuffed with
mushrooms and olives 83-84
petits oignons à la
grecque 52-53
oranges, citrus fruits on
spinach and bean
sprouts 68-69
paella 118-119
pancakes
crêpes aux
poireaux 110-111
crêpes de Noel 230-231
egg bretonne 137
fried rice with hazel
nuts 196-197
passion fruit
soufflés 235-236
pasta and rice 101-128
avocado and rice bean
salad 60-61

bean sprouts and fennel
with egg noodles 166–167
butter bean and rice
cakes 155
Chinese rainbow of
peppers 190–191
coquillettes aux fèves 102
courgette pasta salad in
basil sauce 59–60
crêpes aux
poireaux 110–111
French pea baguette
slice 126–127
fried rice with hazel
nuts 196–197
Indian kedgeree 125
lasagna verdi aux
aubergines 103–104
Macedoine flan 114–115
pilaf aux châtaignes 117
pilaf with saffron 116
polenta gnocchi with
walnuts 106–107
prime pumpkin pie 127–128
ravioli alla Pope 108–109
rice cake 123
risotto verde 124
spaghetti romana new
style 105
Spanish paella 118–119
stuffed peppers 120
tarte de champignons in
brandy sauce 112–113
timbale de riz
parisienne 121
wild rice lentil
casserole 122
pâté
carrot and yoghurt pâté
dip 43
green olive pâté 53–54
hot cheese and potato pâté
with herbs 42
terrine de légumes aux
champignons blancs 156–157
pawpaw pecan
cocktail 54–55
peanuts
African peanut queen
dip 46
nutty brown sauce 29–30
peanut and pumpkin
soup 23
peanut queen dip,
African 46
pears, caramelized apple and
pear tart 212–213

peas see pulses
pecan nuts
celebration pecan pie 246
pawpaw pecan cocktail 54–55
peppers
caponata à la Conil 90–91
Chinese rainbow of
peppers 190–191
mushroom and pepper
moulds 55–56
pepperoni medley 48–49
stuffed peppers 120
tomato piperade 82–83
pilaf
pilaf aux châtaignes 117
pilaf with saffron 116
pine and basil pistou
provencal dip 47
pineapple, coleslaw with
pineapple and cashew
nuts 65–66
pink dressing 34
pistachio nuts
fevettes à la
chinoise 70–71
potato and pistachio
Venetian cakes 180–181
pistou provencal dip, pine and
basil 47
plum sauce 30
polenta gnocchi with
walnuts 106–107
potatoes
artichoke, cucumber and
potato flash 178–179
bean and potato
boxties 159
button sprouts, chestnuts
and new potatoes 182–183
casserole de pommes en
ragôut oriental 172–173
chicory with potato
salad 66–67
clapshot of potato and
swede 170
courge aux pommes
savoyarde 175–176
goulash of potato and onion
in paprika sauce 177–178
gratin des deux pommes
aux amandes 174–175
hot cheese and potato pâté
with herbs 42
new potato salad 64
pomme farcie au fromage
blanc 171

potato and pistachio
Venetian cakes 180-181
tofu medley of aubergine,
potato and celeriac 192-193
pulses
asparagus, bean shoots and
red bean
assortment 194-195
avocado and rice bean
salad 60-61
bean and potato
boxties 159
bean sprouts and fennel
with egg noodles 166-167
broad beans and carrot
custard pie 146-147
butter bean and rice
cakes 155
chickpea and spinach
casserole 154
citrus fruits on spinach and
bean sprouts 68-69
coquillettes aux fèves 102
courge aux
flageolets 164-165
deep fried dwarf beans
milanese 158
fevettes à la
chinoise 70-71
French pea baguette
slice 126-127
galette de petits pois à
la francaise 151
garbanzo beans see chickpeas
haricot verts medley 44-45
hummus (chickpea
caviar) 41
Indian chickpeas and fried
cheese dumplings 162-163
lentil cakes with
chicory 160-161
lentil platter aux petits
légumes 150
Mexican bean
fiesta 152-153
pain de haricot, lentille et
pois vert 167-168
peacock feather fan of
carrots and cucumber 62-63
red bean sauce 31
sweet and sour runner
beans 168
tarte de tomates et haricots
verts nicoise 142-143
tartlets de petits pois et
fromage purée 88-89

terrine de légumes aux
champignons blancs 156-157
wild rice lentil
casserole 122
pumpkins
peanut and pumpkin
soup 23
prime pumpkin pie 127-128
quiche, broccoli and tomato
quiche 138-139
raisins
raisin soup with
yoghurts 19
Swedish raisin sour cake 222
raspberry coulis 206
ratafia biscuits 228
ravioli alla Pope 108-109
rhubarb, apple and rhubarb
mousse 211
rice see pasta and rice
risotto verde 124
Russian fruit kissel 200-201
salad dressings 35
salads
avocado and rice bean
salad 60-61
chicory with potato
salad 66-67
citrus fruits on spinach and
bean sprouts 68-69
coleslaw with pineapple and
cashew nuts 65-66
courgette pasta salad in
basil sauce 59-60
cucumber and mint in
yoghurt dressing 74
fevettes à la
chinoise 70-71
hot mushroom salad 73
new potato salad 64
peacock feather fan of
carrots and cucumber 62-63
pickled cauliflower
salad 71-72
tomato and cucumber in
brandy dressing 58-59
sauces
cheese sauce 27
coconut sauce 28
dairy white sauce 27
egg custard sauce for rich
puddings 205-206
egg sauce 27
lemon sauce 33
Madeira sauce 30
mayonnaise 34-5
mint sauce 35

mushroom sauce 27, 28, 29
nutty brown sauce 29-30
nutty white sauce 28
olive sauce 30
onion sauce 27
pink dressing 34
plain salad cream 35
plum sauce 30
red bean sauce 31
Swedish sauce 35
tartare sauce 34
tomato sauce 32
yoghurt dressing 35
sesame cheesecake 92-93
sherry 37
sherry syllabub 229
sorbets, strawberry sorbet 208
soufflés
French asparagus soufflé
omelette 136-137
passion fruit
soufflés 235-236
soups
apple and beetroot wine
soup 18-19
avocado and tomato
soup 14
beer soup with sweet
onion 22
garlic soup of Provence 20-21
lemon and egg soup 15
Mexican gazpacho with chilli 17
peanut and pumpkin soup 23
raisin soup with yoghurts 19
spaghetti romana new style 105
spinach
carrot and spinach tofu
cakes 94-95
chickpea and spinach
casserole 154
citrus fruits on spinach
and bean sprouts 68-69
Greek cheese and spinach
pie 140-141
poached egg
Florentine 145-146
sponges
birthday sponge cake 218-221
New Year tipsy sponge
savarins 232-234
sprouts, button sprouts,
chestnuts and new
potatoes 182-183
starters
African peanut queen dip 46
asparagus mousse with
toasted almonds 51-52

aubergine caviar 40
baked timbale
d'aubergine 85-86
broccoli beignets 87-88
caponata à la Conil 90-91
carrot and spinach tofu
cakes 94-95
carrot and yoghurt pâté dip 43
Chinese cocktail rolls 96-97
courge aux amandes 77-78
courgette Swiss rarebit 80-81
cream cheese bonne
bouche 76
cream cheese and leek dip 50
green olive pâté 53-54
haricot verts medley 44-45
hot cheese and potato pâté
with herbs 42
hummus (chickpea caviar) 41
Jerusalem artichoke sauté 79
mushroom and pepper
moulds 55-56
onions stuffed with mushrooms
and olives 83-84
pan fried asparagus and
egg cutlets 98-99
pawpaw pecan cocktail 54-55
pepperoni medley 48-49
petits oignons à la
grecque 52-53
pine and basil pistou
provencal dip 47
sesame cheesecake 92-93
tartlets de petits pois et
fromage purée 88-89
tomato piperade 82-83
stir fry dishes
asparagus, bean shoots and red
bean assortment 194-195
broccoli and button
mushrooms 186-187
Chinese rainbow of
peppers 190-191
fried rice with hazel
nuts 196-197
jardiniere de légumes
Cantonese style 188-189
tofu medley of aubergine,
potato and
celeriac 192-193
stollen, festive Austrian 242-243
strawberry sorbet 208
swede, clapshot of potato and
swede 170
Swedish raisin sour cake 222
Swedish sauce 35
tartare sauce 34

timbales
  baked timbale
  d'aubergine 85–86
  timbale de riz parisienne 121
tofu
  carrot and spinach tofu
  cakes 94–95
  tofu medley of aubergine,
  potato and celeriac 192–193
tomatoes
  avocado and tomato soup 14
  baked timbale
  d'aubergine 85–86
  broccoli and tomato
  quiche 138–139
  tarte de tomates et haricots
  verts nicoise 142–143
  tomato and cucumber in
  brandy dressing 58–59
  tomato piperade 82–83
  tomato sauce 32
trifle treasure 224–225
vegetables
  caponata à la Conil 90–91
  casserole de pommes en ragôut
  oriental 172–173
  jardiniere de légumes
  Cantonese style 188–189
  lentil platter aux petits
  légumes 150
  Macedoine flan 114–115
  paella 118–119
  terrine de légumes aux
  champignons blancs 156–157
  see also named varieties
walnuts, polenta gnocchi with
  walnuts 106–107
white sauces 27, 28
wines 37
yoghurt
  carrot and yoghurt pâté dip 43
  cucumber and mint in yoghurt
  dressing 74
  raisin soup with yoghurts 19
  yoghurt dressing 35